IT'S EASY TO

AVOID

PROBATE

by

BARBARA R. STOCK

Linch Publishing, Inc.
1950 Lee Rd.
Winter Park, FL 32789
(or Box 75, Orlando, FL 32802)

PUBLISHED BY:
LINCH PUBLISHING, INC.
1950 LEE RD.
WINTER PARK, FL 32789
(or Box 75, Orlando, FL 32802)

See the back of this book for an order form.

ISBN 0-913455-00-8 Hardbound
Library of Congress Catalog Number: 83-081609
Printed in the U.S.A.

TABLE OF CONTENTS

Important Notice

The author of this book is not an attorney and is not qualified to practice law. All suggestions in this book should be reviewed with your attorney/paralegal. The purpose of this book is to point out the expensive pitfalls of probating an estate and to suggest ways of avoiding probate. Suggested formats for various documents are to illustrate the text and the reader should not attempt to prepare these himself. Again, these should be reviewed with your attorney/paralegal.

It is the author's expectation that this book will forearm the reader so that he or she can be better prepared for the attorney/paralegal-client conference.

All trust formats are samples. "Meant for <u>educational purposes</u> only".

THANK YOU

My Parents—
For their love and support as always

My Friends and Professional Peers—
For reading countless manuscripts and sound advice

INTRODUCTION

Every week in America, approximately $180 million dollars are taken from the pockets of unsuspecting, bereaved families for the expenses of probate — three times the cost of funerals. This is happening because their well-intentioned loved ones, without realizing it and often with expensive legal advice, committed them to an average of 16 months of depressing, tedious, frustrating and extremely costly probate proceedings.

It is my hope that this book will serve as a device in the war against the "legal" plundering of the hard earned assets of America's citizenry by the legal profession. Because many people think probate is inevitable, it is my purpose to provide the information in <u>It's Easy to Avoid Probate</u> to show them positive alternatives.

My knowledge stems from 14 years of experience as a stockbroker with two prestigious member firms of the New York Stock Exchange, Dean Witter Reynolds and Thomson & McKinnon Securities. A stockbroker supervises the transfer of assets (securities) almost daily; someone sells and someone buys.

It is the stockbroker who handles final details in regard to securities for estates. Certificates must have signatures guaranteed since notarization is not acceptable. A signature can be guaranteed <u>only</u> by an officer of a brokerage firm or a bank. A judge or an attorney cannot guarantee a signature on a stock certificate. Because of this technicality, any securities owned by a client's estate had to be submitted to me before final transfer could take place.

Seeing which stock registrations avoided probate and which did not is what caught my attention and inspired me to write this book. Over the years, the "how to's" became familiar and easy. Because I saw the need, I spent 17 months researching every detail of setting up assets to avoid probate court proceedings. This manual is the result.

Even the United States Government has recognized it is preferable to have assets avoid probate.* However, since the states have been left to set up their own systems, unnecessary complexity has resulted. Legislators who are mostly attorneys have passed statutes making probate unnecessarily difficult and time consuming for their own benefit.

*Federal·Register, Vol. 44, No. 248, December 28, 1979:
"The Bureau of Public Debt has pioneered procedures for the disposition of savings...belonging to the estates of deceased owners without requiring probate court proceedings."

In 500 probate court cases studied in nine states, 49 out of 50 estates could have had the majority of their assets avoid probate so the help of an attorney would not have been necessary. The fact that they did not is evidence of the exploitation of public ignorance by the legal profession. It is my intent to provide information to enable you to avoid the legal nightmare called probate.

This book has been written in everyday language, omitting legal terms whenever possible so the nonprofessional person can easily understand the concepts. It has been reviewed by attorneys for accuracy, and all facts and statistics have been thoroughly checked.

Chapter 1

THE AMERICAN MYTH

A popular American myth is that a person's assets avoid probate because he/she has a Will. **Assets held in your name alone at death are like blank pieces of paper.** Cross the name off any deed, title, or bank account because the owner has died and nothing remains to prove ownership. These assets are doomed to probate, with the possible exception of a car and personal belongings.

Let us look at the following illustration to better understand which assets avoid probate and which do not:

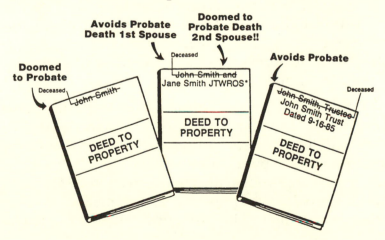

1. Even if you have a perfectly good Will made by an attorney, the first asset must go to probate!

2. The second asset goes to probate, unless changed, at the death of the second spouse!!

In the first deed, or any asset registered only in John Smith's name, a court order is needed to transfer ownership of that asset even if he had a Will. The order must be obtained from the probate court.

In the other two deeds illustrated, Joint Tenancy with Right of Survivorship or the one registered under a trust, the assets avoid probate.

In the case of joint tenancy, **another name is still on the asset** after John Smith's death.

If the asset is registered under a trust as the third deed depicts, **the description of that trust still remains** on the asset after John Smith's death. The trust provides instructions for the distribution of that asset.

I believe the probate court system violates your Constitutional rights. The Fourth Amendment states, "The right of the people to be secure in their . . . papers and effects, against **unreasonable** searches and **seizures***, shall not be violated . . . " The national average of 6% to 22% in probate expenses, depending on the size of the estate, and the average of 16 months time to process the 78% to 94% left violate our guaranteed rights under the Constitution of the United States. These assets have been "confiscated" with little or no access allowed to them by their legal owners, your loved ones.

Webster's Dictionary defines probate as the "proving" of your Will. Often, part of the process to prove your Will is to send out detailed lists of your assets and notices to all interested parties** by certified mail and publish a notice in a newspaper that your Will is being probated. The solution to all the problems of paperwork, expense, and delays of probate is to avoid it. The functions of probate, such as no-

*Author's emphasis
**Interested parties are: 1) relatives who would have been heirs to your assets under your state's laws 2) anyone else named in your Will 3) the person or institution nominated by your Will to be executor 4) creditors - sometimes.

tifying creditors and interested parties, offer little useful service to anyone except attorneys for whom they often produce handsome fees. Let us examine one of these notices:

NOTICE OF ADMINISTRATION

The administration of the estate of Evelyn Sheldon Baxter, deceased, File Number PR 83-1410, is pending in the Circuit Court for Orange County, Florida, Probate Division, the address of which is Orange County Courthouse, Orlando, FL 32801. The name and address of the personal representative and of the personal representative's attorney are set forth below.

ALL CLAIMS AND OBJECTIONS NOT SO FILED WILL BE FOREVER BARRED.

All interested persons are required to file with the court WITHIN THREE MONTHS FROM THE DATE OF THE FIRST PUBLICATION OF THIS NOTICE: (1) all claims against the estate and (2) any objection by an interested person to whom notice was mailed that challenges the validity of the will, the qualifications of the personal representative, venue or jurisdiction of the court.

Date of the first publication of this notice of administration: October 19, 1983.

If assets are left by Will, the detailed information is available to anyone who wishes to review it. Any disgruntled heirs are then allowed from 2 to 9 months (depending on the state) to confer with their attorneys and prepare their case. Notices in a local newspaper are a written invitation to contest your Will. A file was studied in which a maid contested the Will. The court records are full of such ridiculous cases. Using recommendations given in this book, suits like this would be almost nonexistent.

Every asset which has a piece of paper as evidence of ownership can be registered to avoid probate, and so can other assets such as diamonds, livestock, furniture, etc. It is all a matter of knowing. Without the key, it is very difficult to enter your house, but with the key, it becomes very easy. This book will provide you the "**key**" to have your assets avoid probate.

My associates and I studied 500 probate court files drawn at random in nine states. Approximately 8% of the cases were still open when studied. The average time calculated from these files to close an estate was 16 months, a figure on the low side because of these open cases. However, this figure is representative of the majority.

In 370 of the 500 files studied, we were able to verify (or reasonably estimate) the costs of probate, an average of $7,800 for all estates probated. A table is given in Chapter 4 of the average percentages for various size estates, which will give a more accurate estimate of the possible cost. For example, for estates of $5,000 or less, it costs an average of 22% of the assets or $1,100!

Money that goes for expenses of probate is money that does not go to your loved ones. It goes, for the most part to attorneys, who make an average of $4,500 in fees per estate. These fees average **4.1%** of the assets that go through probate. **The legal profession should be congratulated for finding a way to legally get 4.1% of the life savings of the majority of Americans.**[1] It is completely unnecessary in 49 out of 50 cases with the right advice and planning. That "right" advice is often not given by attorneys for their own gain. Granted, some attorneys do not know the "how to's" of avoiding probate, a serious shortcoming of their education!

Some attorneys argue that the court's supervision will "protect" your assets and assure they are distributed as you

---

[1]The average includes **all** attorneys' fees charged to any one estate. Fees can be paid to several attorneys from an estate. One attorney can handle the legal work, a second act as executor, and yet a third be needed to execute probate proceedings of assets held in another state.

wish. How can this be true when our study verified that the first 6% to 22% goes to the cost of probate? **That is up to 1/5 or more of what many have worked a lifetime to accumulate!**

This book gives the advantages and disadvantages of joint ownership and of assets held under a trust, the two primary ways to avoid probate. A chapter is also provided on each type of asset since each has its own peculiarities on how to be set up to avoid probate. This is the first complete handbook on the subject.

Arizona is one of 14 states that has passed the Uniform Probate Code, which supposedly simplifies probate proceedings.[2] A pamphlet published by the Scottsdale Bar Association says that the proceedings can be lengthy and complex when assets must be probated, **even if the individual had a Will**.[3] **Any time** one gets involved in a court system, it is costly and time consuming.

How can anything be simple when it takes **six** months before assets can be distributed? So much for the Uniform Probate Code.

[2]The minimum time period before any assets can be distributed in all 14 states which have enacted their own version of the Uniform Probate Code is an average of 4 months plus the time required for the attorney to prepare and file the necessary paperwork. Since the time to process the paperwork to open and then to close an estate takes at least 2 months, in reality the minimum time is 6 months. This is for any estate over approximately $5,000 which is subject to all the burdens and costs of regular probate, (<u>Washington Post</u>, Article: "Settling Estates Still Needlessly Complex," Jane Bryant Quinn, August 4, 1983.) In some states, the limit can be as low as $500 or it can be as high as $30,000 with the average being $5,000. The heirs to estates under the limit can go to the probate court, and the clerks will help them with the paperwork. No attorney is necessary.

[3]<u>Fables & Fallacies About Wills & Probate</u>, 1977, Scottsdale Bar Association, Arizona.

If the advice of this book is taken, assets can be distributed as soon as a death certificate and necessary state inheritance tax waivers are available, which is often only a few days.

Soon after becoming a stockbroker, two of my clients died. One estate went through probate and it took two and a half years. The other estate had its securities and other assets registered under a trust. It took only a week to settle. After being bogged down with the paperwork caused by a court system on the first estate, I vowed this was the last time any of my clients' assets would go through probate. I made myself familiar with how to avoid it.

Chapter 2

PROBATE CAN EASILY BE AVOIDED

Probate can be avoided if assets are registered in joint ownership, which is probably appropriate for one-half or more of the people reading this book. Since the change in the federal estate tax laws in 1981, it has become much more attractive for many (Chapter 7 should be read before re-registering any asset to joint ownership). Most of the material on the subject prior to this book has been written by attorneys, who are usually negative towards joint ownership. Attorneys have a vested interest in seeing that your assets do not avoid probate — **their fees**.

For those who feel that joint ownership is not appropriate, there is a solution. It is called the **SIMPLE BENEFICIARY TRUST**. With a Simple Beneficiary Trust (also a living trust), **you are your own trustee** and continue to manage your assets as you always have. **There are no administrative fees**. Instead of your executor, your successor trustee carries out your wishes.

A trust, and the fact that it avoids probate, is one of the best kept secrets of the legal profession. It enables the settlement of an estate to become a family affair without court intervention. If problems arise, it is an ironclad legal document that heirs can ask the court to enforce. You give instructions while you are living for disposition of your assets and this is why it is called a "living trust." It is the way Bing Crosby, Jack Kennedy, and John Lennon left their assets to their heirs. John Lennon left an estimated $100-$200 million dollars.[4] If such prominent and well advised people use a trust to pass large sums of money to their heirs, so can you.

Only one type of asset cannot avoid probate; miscellaneous checks issued shortly before or just after your death in your name. The best planning cannot prevent this from occurring. You need a Will to make provisions for these checks. If all other assets avoid probate, the amount of these checks (such as a last social security check, refund of a utility deposit, and reimbursement of medical expenses) will, in 49 out of 50 cases, fall below your state's limit where the services of an attorney are needed.

Would you dream of not having a beneficiary on a life insurance policy? Of course not. That is **exactly** what you are doing by having **any** asset registered only in your name. If you have no beneficiary designated on a life insurance policy or the beneficiary has died, the proceeds must go through probate just like assets registered **only** in your name. **A beneficiary can now be designated for all your assets with a Simple Beneficiary Trust almost as easily as designating a beneficiary on a life insurance policy.**

The Simple Beneficiary Trust is written, for the most part, in easy to understand language. Some legal terms are used with specific intent; for example, under Trust Name, the word Grantor is used. The reason is that a recent IRS ruling that waives some paperwork required for a trust uses this terminology. If your tax advisor reads your trust, it might be helpful to use the same terminology as the IRS ruling.

Every single Will examined in hundreds of probate court records said, "I nominate, appoint and constitute

---

[4]Trusts & Estates Magazine, March, 1983, p. 63.

XYZ as my executor." This is unnecessary legal language — "I appoint" is sufficient. Court approval of the executor named in a Will is required to determine the person's competency to handle the estate.

It is time the American public is provided with legal documents written in clear and concise English. The unnecessary and confusing language used in many legal documents can obscure the most basic ideas.

Persons who are 1) single 2) widowed with more than one child to share in their assets or 3) married but with separate property will probably find a Simple Beneficiary Trust the best way to have assets avoid probate.

Here are the first few paragraphs of a Simple Beneficiary Trust to help you better understand this method of setting up assets to avoid probate (complete format included in Chapter 8):

I, John C. Smith, a resident of St. Louis County, Minnesota and being of sound mind, make this Trust Agreement and revoke any Trust Agreements I previously executed, and any amendments to these prior Trust Agreements.

1. <u>Trust Purpose</u>: The purpose of this Trust is to hold all assets owned by this Trust for the benefit of John C. Smith's wife, Jane B. Smith. If Jane B. Smith is deceased or unwilling to receive the assets owned by this Trust, then the beneficiary shall be the children of John C. and Jane B. Smith to share equally in the assets owned by this Trust. If any child is deceased or unwilling to receive their share of the assets owned by this Trust, then that child's children shall share equally in what would have been that child's share.

John C. Smith may use the principal and income from assets owned by this Trust for as long as he lives at his sole discretion. Jane B. Smith if she becomes the Successor Trustee may use the principal and income from the assets owned by this trust at her sole discretion for her support, general welfare, health, and education. A Successor Trustee is provided if John C. Smith and/or Jane B. Smith are incapacitated as defined herein. At the death of John C. Smith and Jane B. Smith, all the assets of this Trust are to be distributed and this Trust terminates.

It is to any Successor Trustee's sole discretion to distribute any personal possessions of John C. and Jane B. Smith at their death or in the event they should be incapacitated.

2.   Trust Name and Property: This Trust Agreement shall be known as the "John C. Smith Trust Dated March 22, 1983." Any asset which bears the registration "John C. Smith, Trustee Under John C. Smith Trust Dated 3-22-83" or an abbreviated version of this shall be governed by this Trust. John C. Smith is the Grantor (Owner) and Trustee. John C. Smith has executed all the instructions separately in writing to transfer and deliver to the Trustee all his assets to be held by this Trust according to the terms as specified herein.

3.   Successor Trustee: If John C. Smith is incapacitated as certified in writing by two licensed physicians or is deceased, the Successor Trustee shall be Jane B. Smith, his wife. If she is deceased or unable or unwilling to serve, then John C. Smith, Jr., his son, shall be Successor Trustee. It is to any Successor Trustee's sole discretion to distribute any personal possessions of John C. Smith and/or Jane B. Smith. The Successor Trustee agrees to serve with no compensation unless it is agreed to by all the beneficiaries.

The Trustee or any Successor Trustee may use any net income and any principal of the assets owned by this Trust which he/she deems best for the health, education, support, and general welfare of John C. Smith and/or Jane B. Smith in a manner of living to which they are accustomed. The Successor Trustee may also add to income and/or principal, or make changes in the investments of this Trust at his/her sole and absolute discretion.

I suggest the final draft of the Simple Beneficiary Trust be drawn for you by an attorney/paralegal. A beautifully typed, properly witnessed, and notarized legal document provides assurance to your heirs that these were your last wishes and facilitates your wishes being carried out.

Chapter 3

PROBATE:
A SYSTEM DESIGNED BY ATTORNEYS
FOR THE BENEFIT OF ATTORNEYS

The American Bar Association Journal had a cartoon in a recent issue:

*"I had a nightmare last night. I dreamt
everything was settled out of court."*

Reprinted by permission of Joseph Farris, cartoonist

This cartoon says it all as to why the legal profession does little to help the American public set up their assets to avoid probate.

The Bar Association reports that only 30% of Americans have a Will, although the high risk group, the elderly and those in poor health, do have Wills made before their death. In 3 out of 4 probate court records surveyed in our study, the person had a Will made by an attorney. Yet, their assets had to be processed through probate, despite the fact that an attorney was consulted. Why?

We have 389,000[5] medical doctors and 617,000[6] attorneys in practice. Many people need the services of an attorney only at 3 or 4 points during their whole lifetime. Many of those same people see a doctor 3 or 4 times a year. Yet, there are far more attorneys than there are doctors.

In 1981, 42,383 new members were admitted to the Bar, and 129,739 were enrolled in law school.[7] By 1984 there will be nearly 700,000 attorneys complicating your life. The number of attorneys has increased by 83% in the last 10 years. At the present rate law schools are conferring degrees, the number of attorneys will double in the next 10 years. That will make their numbers almost quadrupling in a 20 year period!

Warren Burger, Chief Justice of the U.S. Supreme Court has been quoted, "We may be on our way to a society overrun by hordes of lawyers hungry as locusts."

[5]Physician Characteristics and Distribution in the U.S., 1982 p. 64, American Medical Association.

[6]American Bar Association Membership Report, November, 1982.

[7]A Review of Legal Education in the U.S. — 1981-82, published by the American Bar Association.

The United States has more attorneys than the entire rest of the world put together. For instance in Japan, a society almost as sophisticated and complex as ours, there are 9,750 people for every attorney. In the United States there are only 370 people for every attorney.[8] **We have twenty-five (25) times more attorneys per person than Japan.**

It is to the advantage of the attorneys to maintain an appearance of complexity and to find a way to drag these probate proceedings out. It is not necessary. In England, it costs 1/100 as much to probate an estate as in the United States and takes 1/17 the amount of time. In Germany, probate is almost automatic.[9] If an attorney probates only his "share" of estates a year, approximately 2.2 at $4,500 each, his average income from these fees is $9,900 annually! Since many attorneys specialize and never probate an estate, he probably probates twice that many or 4.4, giving him $19,800 a year from this source or almost $1 million during his career.[10]

The American legal profession is basically an overcrowded field. I attribute many of the abuses I discovered in probate to the fact that there is not enough work to support all the attorneys, so they must create work.

[8]This is based on the 1982 estimate of the United States population of 230.2 million (World Almanac & Book of Facts, 1983, page 954) and the estimate of 617,320 attorneys.

[9]HALT (Help Abolish Legal Tyranny), a nonprofit, tax exempt organization, 201 Mass. Ave., N.E., Ste. 319, Washington, D.C. 20002. We recommend this organization — 1 year membership — donation of $15.00 or more.

[10]The 2.2 figure is derived as follows: approximately 1% of the population dies annually; 1% x 370 people per attorney = 3.7 x 60% = 2.2 (60% have assets probated). $19,800 x 40 years = $792,000 (assuming he becomes an attorney at age 25 and works until age 65).

Attorneys make the laws, and a thorough study of many states' laws soon reveals how they have designed the probate system for their own benefit. Take, for example, the order in which the various bills and obligations must be paid from an estate. In most states, the attorneys' fees must be paid first,[11] before any allowance can be made to the family, before the doctors and hospital can be paid for their services during a last illness, and even the funeral director.

Attorneys often argue that probate is necessary to protect creditors. Our study revealed that of the few bills filed (an average of six) with the probate court, most are minor as a large percentage of last illness bills are paid by medical insurance (there might be only $70 owed to the hospital, $28 to the doctor). Yet, these same creditors often pay fees and are forced to do an inordinate amount of paperwork to file claims with the probate court. Heirs are responsible for your bills only to the extent that they have received assets from your estate — not for an unlimited amount.

Let us examine an actual probate court case to see how stacked the deck is:

Priority of Payment of Claims:
Statute 733.707

Cash Balance on Hand: **$4,191.50**

CLASS 1: Expenses to administer the estate and **THE ATTORNEYS' FEES**

ATTORNEY'S FEE	$1,600.00
Court Filing Fee & Misc.	299.39
Personal Representative Fee	111.00
TOTAL:	$2,010.39

CLASS 2: Funeral, interment, and grave marker expenses. Maximum allowed $1,500.

The Guardian Memorial Chapel	$1,500.00

CLASS 3: Taxes.   -0-

CLASS 4: Medical expenses of the last illness of the decedent.

Name	Amount Owed	Pro-rated (52%
L. Smith, M.D.	$ 129.00	$ 66.49
Hospital	146.00	75.36
Cardiology Assoc.	1046.00	539.26
	$1321.00	$681.11

CASH BALANCE: -0-

CLASS 5: FAMILY ALLOWANCE   -0-
(Maximum $6,000)

CLASS 6: All other claims.   -0-

PAID TO HEIRS   **-0-**

If there had been no expenses to probate this estate, there would have been $1,371 left for this man's daughter and 100% of the hospital and doctors' bills would have been paid. This man would probably roll over in his grave if he knew his daughter did not get a cent, but the attorney got $1,600, and only 52% of the bills for his last illness had been paid. Nowhere in this man's Will did it state, "I leave $1,600 to the attorney."

So much for the attorneys' argument that probate is necessary to insure that creditors are paid. **The primary ones it protects are attorneys. In the majority of cases where there were insufficient funds to pay creditors, there would have been enough to pay all the bills if no fees had been paid to attorneys.**

Attorneys often charge what they think the "traffic will bear," or what the state's statutes will allow. In some states, the statutes permit a percentage to be charged that depends on the size of the estate. These laws are passed by attorneys for the benefit of attorneys. Fees are often excessive in comparison to the amount of work done and the time attorneys spend on estates.

Unless a specific percentage is allowed by the statutes, the court usually considers the attorney's fee negotiable between the executor and the attorney employed on behalf of the estate. The court will not intervene unless an heir objects, even if the charges appear to be excessive.

If an objection is made, in many states a judge decides if the fee is reasonable based on statements from two other attorneys who, in many cases, are friends of the one submitting the bill! An heir could retaliate by obtaining affidavits that the fee was unreasonable from a third and fourth attorney. He must pay yet **another** attorney to petition for a hearing and represent him. The heir might have to spend $1,000 to ask that a bill be reduced by $1,000. If he wins the argument, at best he might break even.

In terms of **time** and **stress**, the only place in our judicial system I have seen the rich get treated poorly is in probate. The poor tend to sail through; the rich have it drag on for years. Paperwork and proceedings serve to continuously bring back painful memories. Money, in this case, often **buys** being led down the Primrose Path to the probate court by what might have been a trusted legal advisor in **all** other aspects of life. As his retirement looms, the attorney's judgement is clouded by the financial security that handling your estate, and those of others, will provide. To quote an attorney who is a friend of mine, "Probate is the only **easy** money I have ever made practicing law."

The public has been at the mercy of attorneys far too long. Attorneys frequently do not take an estate through the most efficient statutes provided. The longer and more complicated the proceedings, the larger the fee attorneys can probably charge. For example, in Maryland we found one estate that had gone through probate with only two 1974 cars worth approximately $1300. This man left everything to his wife in his Will. If his wife had gone to the Register of Wills[12] first, she would have found out she needed only one form, which follows, signed by the Register of Wills certifying there was no inheritance tax due. The Department of Transportation would then have registered those two car titles as she requested.

[12]"Register" (rather than "Registrar") of Wills is used throughout the book due to the fact that several states use it on their stationery and forms. Registrar is the correct term today, but 100 or more years ago when these offices were established, Register was probably correct.

Maryland Department of Transportation MOTOR VEHICLE ADMINISTRATION 6601 RITCHIE HIGHWAY, N.E. GLEN BURNIE, MARYLAND 21062	CERTIFICATION OF LEGAL HEIR	THE OPERATOR'S LICENSE OF THE DECEDENT MUST ACCOMPANY THIS CERTIFICATION

I, _____ , whose relationship to _____
NAME OF LEGAL HEIR   NAME OF DECEDENT

the decedent is: (CHECK APPLICABLE BLOCK BELOW)

☐ Surviving spouse with children ☐ Surviving spouse without minor children ☐ Other heir _____
RELATIONSHIP

do hereby state, that the vehicle described below is the only personal property left by the decedent and the vehicle is transferable to my name under the provisions of Section 5-608, Estates and Trust Article of the Annotated Code of Maryland. I further state that I have notified all other legal heirs, whose names I have listed below, and they have relinquished all rights and interest in the vehicle. I also state that all debts and taxes of the decedent have been paid.

YEAR	MAKE	MODEL	BODY STYLE	VEHICLE IDENTIFICATION NUMBER

YOU MUST LIST ALL OTHER LEGAL HEIRS ON THE LINES BELOW

_____
_____
_____
_____
_____
_____
_____

I certify, under Penalty of perjury, that the statements made herein are true and correct, to the best of my knowledge, information and belief.

_____ ☐ LS
SIGNATURE OF LEGAL HEIR

Witness my Hand and Seal

This _____ day of _____ 19____

TO BE COMPLETED BY REGISTER OF WILLS

I the undersigned, the Register of Wills in and for the County of _____ in the State of Maryland do hereby certify that satisfactory evidence of death for the decedent named above has been presented to me. I also certify that the decedent died; ☐ leaving a will, which has been filed at this office ☐ intestate. I further certify that the inheritance tax; ☐ has been paid in the amount of $_____ covering the vehicle described above ☐ is not due.

_____
SIGNATURE OF REGISTER OF WILLS

VR-90 (7-82)

Unfortunately, she went to an attorney first. The total cost was several hundred dollars instead of zero. It took 4 months and 16 pages of legal work. **I found the practice of not taking estates through the most efficient statutes allowed occurred as frequently as 1 in 5 cases.** The Register of Wills said she knew that every single page of the 16 was unnecessary. However, she did not think it was up to her to question the attorney. As a result, she and many others take unnecessary paperwork from attorneys and say nothing. The probate court judge is the one who should have done the questioning.

The judge should also prevent excessive fees in 50% or more of cases that go through probate. He appears to sign whatever probate forms are necessary, and sends the cases back to be filed. Rarely do judges raise questions about **any** fees charged to an estate. The layman is mislead into thinking he is "protected" because the estate is going through a judicial system. Considering that 6% to 22% of assets disappear to the expense of probate, how much protection can there be?

A person is as helpless as a patient under general anesthesia when assets must be probated. Fortunately, doctors are kinder with their scalpels than attorneys and banks are at slicing away estate assets.

Here is a case drawn at random in the course of the study done of probate court records:

Assets	$7,891
Bank's Fee as Executor	- 3,000
Attorney's Fee	- 750
Other Probate Expenses	- 185
Debts Paid	- 1,818
Misc.	- 149
Interest Income	+ 385
NET LEFT TO HEIR	**$2,374**

You will note the estate had $7,891 of which the heir received only $2,374. The gentleman had a perfectly good Will, and everything went as smooth as silk, so how could this have happened?

This man lived in low income housing for the last few years of his life. It was probably only with considerable effort he held on to his savings which in his Will, he stated that he wished his step-daughter to receive — not the bank and the attorney.

There were $1,818 of debts paid for the decedent. The trust company that was executor charged a flat fee of $3,000. The attorney did not take the estate through the most efficient statutes allowed. His fee, instead of perhaps $150, was $750. This also caused the filing fee to be higher and ads were necessary. The bank and attorney received $3,750 — the step-daughter $2,374!

Forty-eight percent (48%) of the estate went into the coffers of the bank and into the attorney's pockets. A total of more than 50% disappeared. The court, a bank, and an attorney were all there "protecting" these assets. Protection like this we can all live without.

If you have a friend who is a newspaper reporter, tell him/her that we would appreciate hearing from them. We have a package to send to newspaper reporters to help them develop a story to expose the numerous abuses of probate going on in his/her area. My time, and that of several employees of my publisher, is devoted to answering phone calls of reporters and consumer groups. We tell them what to look for. There is enough material for a four or five part series right in their own back yard — their

I have five books written by attorneys for attorneys on how to make money at practicing law - they all say the same thing - just make a Will for them and your rewards will come! One out of three families lose 10% to 15% or more of their life savings to the cost of probate but hardly a word has been said about it in the press. You need to study the "unregulated monster" called probate yourself by examining at my direction approximately 50 probate court cases at your local county probate court and see it with your own eyes. I warn you, it will take at least a week of your time but I promise you an award winning story in return! Just call the toll free number below or send a note to the below address to receive your free package to develop the story of the year!

U.S. 1-800-327-7055

Fla. 1-800-432-0399

Linch Publishing, Box 75, Orlando, Fl. 32802.

Please include the reporter's name, the name of the publication, and the phone number with the request.

Chapter 4

WHAT IS THE COST OF PROBATE?

So far this book has given you only averages. For all the cases included in the study, the average cost of probate is $7,800 with the average in assets probated per estate $110,000. This chapter contains a table to calculate the cost of probating your assets, depending on amounts involved, which will be more specific to your needs.

The costs used to compile the schedule in this chapter were taken from actual expenses contained in probate court files. If anything was missing such as the attorney's fee, a letter was written for verification of the missing expense figure. Estimates were used for a very minor percentage of the total costs, and this was done only when the estimate could be accurately made. A typical example is an estimate of the costs of ads that notified creditors and all heirs the estate was being probated. All of the ads in any one state used the same wording. Many files would have the cost of the ad, and this made it easy to determine this expense.

Some of these ads were up to eight inches long, costing hundreds of dollars. None of this is required if you do not have anything probated, or have only minimal assets so the amount falls below your state's minimum for Disposition without Administration (Small Estate).

Estimate the value of assets held only in your name that could be probated. Then multiply by the applicable percentage given in this table:

Table 1

Cost to Probate Various Size Estates

0	—	$ 5,000	22.0%
5,001	—	10,000	14.0%
10,001	—	25,000	11.0%
25,001	—	50,000	7.2%
50,001	—	100,000	6.5%
100,001	—	200,000	6.4%
200,001	—	300,000	6.3%
300,001	—	up	6.2%

NOTE: Approximately 60% to attorneys, 40% to executors and other costs — 98% of which is unnecessary.

Persons having assets of $90,000 that must be probated will pay 6.5% or $5,850 in average probate costs. It is a waste to have assets registered only in your name making them destined for probate court! Remember, any court system is going to be costly and time consuming no matter how efficiently it is run.

One attorney pointed out the figures in the study could be too high because some costs might be attributed to assets not probated. These figures were documented in the case files and that portion of the fee was omitted from the study. In every case where an executor's fee was awarded on a percentage basis, the file showed the total amount of assets on which the fee was calculated. For example, the court might award an executor's fee of $12,000, when $100,000 in assets were probated. The fee would appear to be 12%. However, the file would also reflect that the executor distributed assets of $200,000 that were not probated or a total of $300,000. Therefore, the fee of $12,000 was only 4%. In this case, only $4,000 (100,000 x 4%) could be counted as an expense of probate. This attorney had obviously never looked at a large number of probate court files closely or he would know this argument is invalid.

Printed below are the estimates of expenses of probate from a table published in How to Avoid Probate. The author of this book told me he obtained this table from a Kiplinger Newsletter published shortly before the first edition of his book went to press in 1966. This same table is in his updated edition in 1983. Despite the fact that 1/3 of the states by now have passed the Uniform Probate Code and most other states have enacted at least part of it, the costs are only minutely less. According to attorneys, the Uniform Probate Code was suppose to substantially decrease these costs. So much for the Uniform Probate Code brought about by the first book on the topic of avoiding probate. There are not any figures given for estates under $50,000. No matter which table you use, the cost of probate is invariably expensive.

Table 2

1960's Cost of Probate

$50,000	—	$100,000	7.8%
100,000	—	200,000	7.2%
200,000	—	300,000	6.8%
300,000	—	400,000	6.5%
400,000	—	500,000	6.3%

Chapter 5

ESTATE PLANNING

Estate planning is defined as providing for the efficient passage of assets at your death to those you chose, providing for the support of dependents, and making the necessary plans to minimize death taxes. I define probate costs as a "death tax." My study revealed this "tax" is more costly in most cases than death taxes paid to the government and funeral expenses combined. Plans need to be made so it will not be levied against your estate.

PROBATE

TAX
COLLECTOR - $1,105 STATE
(FEDERAL - 0 IF UNDER)

1984: $325,000
1985:   400,000
1986:   500,000
1987:   600,000

AVERAGE COST OF
PROBATE: $7,800

FUNERAL
$3,000

There are some other basics to estate planning that you need to understand. One is to determine if you are subject to federal estate and/or gift taxes. You do not need to worry about **either** if your total assets fall below the following:

TABLE 3

1984	$325,000
1985	$400,000
1986	$500,000
1987	$600,000

The higher exemptions will help joint ownership become much more popular (Chapter 7).

If all assets are left to a spouse, there is no federal estate tax even if you leave them millions of dollars as per the 1981 Economic Recovery Tax Act (unlimited marital deduction). However, taxes would be due at the death of the remaining spouse if assets exceed the above amounts. Federal estate taxes are based on the sum total of all your assets at death, including proceeds of life insurance if you were the owner of the policy. Life insurance proceeds are not subject to federal income tax. They are subject to a last donation at the Pearly Gate: federal estate tax; an IRS agent is standing there with a basket.

No matter how much you have in assets, even over $600,000, it is advisable to have those assets avoid probate. As mentioned in Chapter 2, John Lennon left $100 to $200 million, and **none** of his assets went through probate. He knew how to do it!

There could be taxes due at the death of the remaining spouse when the total assets are over $600,000 by 1987, or as pointed out in Table 3. You need tax advice if your assets are at or over the limits taxable or might be in the near future. There are many good books written on the subject of how to minimize federal estate taxes. One is offered at the back of this book. You can also find help from your tax advisor and your other financial advisors.

Understand the basics of estate planning before going to an attorney and have the information he needs organized, as you are prepared when going to your tax advisor. Do not assume everything will be "all right" because you have seen an attorney. See that your assets are registered to avoid probate. Remember, our study showed that 3 out of 4 people with assets that went through probate had a Will made by an attorney. These people had gotten professional advice on estate planning, but still an average of 6% to 22% of their assets were lost.

In 1981, legislation was passed that liberalized federal estate taxes. Assets registered in joint tenancy after 1981 are taxed 50% in the marriage partner's estate. Prior to legislation in 1976, unless the surviving spouse could prove ownership of assets, 100% was taxed at the death of the first spouse, and 100% again at the death of the second. This resulted in double taxation. "Proof of contribution" is no longer necessary. In 1981 further legislation was passed, allowing an unlimited amount to be given to one's spouse in his lifetime or at death.

The old rule still holds true for others owning property jointly that are not married. For example, a mother and daughter hold assets in joint ownership, and the daughter dies. The mother would have to be able to prove the assets were paid for solely by her to avoid them being taxed in the daughter's estate. However, since the exemptions as in Table 3 are higher, joint ownership will not cause any federal estate tax to be due in most cases. Prior to 1976, when the first liberalizing legislation was passed, federal estate taxes were levied on estates over $60,000, not $600,000 as scheduled in 1987.

Tax planning for assets over the taxable amount can be accomplished by another version of the Simple Beneficiary Trust. If assets avoid probate, many difficulties to settle an estate disappear and a corporate trustee is rarely necessary. If a corporate trustee is indicated in your case, you should shop for one carefully. Read Chapter 25 on appointing a successor trustee and executor.

When you keep good records, most tax advisors should be able to prepare your federal estate and/or state inheritance tax returns. No federal estate tax return has to be filed if assets fall below the amount taxable. Personnel of state inheritance tax departments told me attorneys frequently file unnecessary paperwork with them. Consult your CPA or tax advisor on these matters. Hopefully, they will be more efficient in determining what is "necessary."

Many states have estate or inheritance taxes. Almost half of the states have no separate inheritance tax if the amount of assets falls below the amount taxable for federal estate taxes. These states are: Alabama, Alaska, Arizona, Arkansas, California, Colorado, Florida, Georgia, Hawaii, Illinois, Maine*, Minnesota, Missouri, Montana**, Nevada, New Mexico, North Dakota, Oregon***, Texas, Utah, Vermont, Virginia, Washington, and Wyoming. See Chapter 22 and seek local advice before you transfer or re-register any assets. If your assets are over the amount not subject to federal estate tax, consult your tax and other financial advisors.

*Maine's inheritance tax will be phased out by July 1, 1986, leaving only the Federal Credit.

**Nonlineal descendants (aunts, uncles, nieces, nephews, and cousins) are not eligible for as high an exemption.

***Oregon's state tax will be phased out January 1, 1987, leaving only the Federal Credit.

A trust is easy to compose when no planning for federal estate taxes must be done. **Trusts have always been possible.** They have been around since the days of the Romans and are well entrenched in legal precedent. Attorneys do not want to make them unless forced to for minimizing federal estate taxes. Then, they will set up what is called a testamentary trust via your Will, dooming assets to probate **before** they can be placed in the trust.

Get pencil and paper and use the following form to calculate the value of your assets. It will only take a few minutes. Take inventory of your assets periodically. How can you plan on where you want to go if you do not know where you are? Having helped hundreds with this form, and working on it for years, I have made it easy to complete. Tax limits are now so high before any federal estate or gift tax is due, that estimates are usually good enough. This form will also provide you with a checklist to make sure all your assets have been set up to avoid probate.

(See Appendix II for tear out Asset Sheet)

ASSET SHEET

Name _____ Date _____

1. FIXED ASSETS

	Amount	Name(s) Held In*
Any excess in checking account	_____	_____
Passbook Savings	_____	_____
Money Market Fund	_____	_____
Money Market Fund	_____	_____
Certificates of Deposit	_____	_____
Certificates of Deposit	_____	_____
Credit Union Accounts	_____	_____
U.S. Savings Bonds	_____	_____
Corporate Bonds/Trusts	_____	_____
Ginnie Mae/Trusts	_____	_____
Tax Exempt Bonds/Trusts	_____	_____
U.S. Treasury or Federal Agency Bonds	_____	_____
Mortgages	_____	_____
Miscellaneous	_____	_____

TOTAL 1.   _____

2. LIFE INSURANCE & ANNUITIES

	Amount	Beneficiary	Age**
Life Insurance-			
Husband	_____	_____	_____
Wife	_____	_____	_____
Annuities	_____	_____	_____

TOTAL 2.   _____

*Single name or only in one name — please list whose name, joint ownership (be sure not tenancy in common), "**IN TRUST FOR**" at banks or savings & loans, or under your own trust agreement.
**Only to make sure beneficiaries are over 18.
   If under 18, see Chapter 23

3. <u>VARIABLE ASSETS</u>

	Cost	Market Value	Name(s) Held In
Real Estate (net equity in home; market value minus mortgage)	_____	_____	_____
Other real estate (net equity)	_____	_____	_____
Real Estate Partnerships	_____	_____	_____
	_____	_____	_____

TOTAL 3. _____   _____

4. <u>STOCKS & BONDS</u>

Name of Company	No. of Shares	Cost Basis	Market Value	Name(s) Held In
_____	_____	_____	_____	_____
_____	_____	_____	_____	_____
_____	_____	_____	_____	_____
_____	_____	_____	_____	_____
_____	_____	_____	_____	_____

TOTAL 4. _____   _____

5. <u>MISCELLANEOUS</u>

Retirement Plans: Laws concerning these are complex. To determine your total amount of assets, include the entire amount in your retirement plans. If this places you at or near the estate tax limit, seek advice on the portion that would be includable for federal estate and/or state inheritance taxes.

Retirement Plans   _____

	Cost	Market Value	Name(s) Held In
Cars	_____	_____	_____
Value of business or practice	_____	_____	_____
Personal property (jewelry, furniture, etc.)	_____	_____	_____
Other	_____	_____	_____
TOTAL 5.	_____	_____	

TOTAL ESTIMATED ASSETS:

	COST	MARKET VALUE
(Add 1, 2, 3, 4, and 5)	_____	_____

If your total assets fall **below** the amounts exempt from federal estate taxes, you can also give everything away before your death and pay no gift tax. The only advantage to utilizing the $10,000 annual gift exclusion is if assets are (or potentially will be) over the limits for federal estate taxes. If you have no income, the $1,000 personal exemption for federal income tax is of no benefit to you, likewise, the $10,000 exclusion for gift tax.

EXAMPLE SITUATIONS

Example 1: A mother has $325,000 in assets registered in her name alone. She re-registers these assets with a son in Joint Tenancy with Right of Survivorship. Since $325,000 is exempt from both federal and/or gift taxes in 1984, she has no liability. She has technically given away $162,500 (1/2) as a gift to her son by re-registering these assets in Joint Tenancy with Right of Survivorship. In theory, the son now owns half the assets.

Example 2: This woman leaves the $325,000 by her Will or by a Simple Beneficiary Trust. Her son's cost basis for the total amount of assets will be eligible for the "stepped-up" basis, the value of assets as of the date of her death. It is amazing the number of attorneys who insist on probating estates for this eligibility **when a trust provides the same advantage**.

Example 3: Should this same woman have a home she purchased for $50,000 which is now worth $175,000, there is $125,000 in appreciated value. Long-term capital gains tax could be completely escaped on this $125,000 if left by a Simple Beneficiary Trust or by Will to her children. The net effect with joint ownership would be that only 1/2 of the profit would be exempt from the long-term capital gains tax. Remember 1/2 is owned by the joint tenant still living.

Attorneys like to allude to the tax pitfalls of joint ownership — scare tactics on their part. There are very few people who use joint ownership who will be penalized by extra taxes with the recent changes in federal estate tax law **or** because assets have increased in value. There is a one time exemption of $125,000 on the profit on the sale of a home-stead if you are over age 55. A home is usually the primary asset. For most married couples, the "stepped-up" basis does not apply. The spouse will probably be over 55 before the "principal residence" is sold, so there would be no capital gains tax to pay if the profit is $125,000 or less.

Individuals with assets which have increased in value, see your tax advisor. He will know your tax status and possible future tax bracket far better than an attorney. His fee is usually less to consult with you on an hourly basis. A CPA charges $35 to $50 an hour for consultation. A few complicated cases will need the help of an attorney who is also a specialist in this area. Before going to see either, order The Handbook of Estate Planning offered at the back of this book so that a minimum amount of his time will be required.

Attorneys fail to mention that you can often save inheritance taxes in some states by the use of joint ownership. For example, in Michigan, any jointly owned property is exempt from state inheritance tax if the property had been held this way at least two years prior to death. This might make joint ownership the best decision for a parent with only one child in that state. Similar savings can be obtained in Maryland, Pennsylvania, and Washington, D.C..

For residents of states where inheritance tax will be due, read Chapter 22. This chapter will give you a general idea of these taxes and a list of questions to ask when making a phone call to your state's inheritance tax office.

Consult your tax advisor if there is any likelihood that you will inherit or accumulate substantial assets in the near future which will make your total assets exceed the amount not subject to federal estate taxes. For all others, do not worry about it. If you hold a million dollar lottery ticket, or discover oil in the backyard, you can afford to have your tax advisor and attorney make some fancy estate plans quickly.

A remote possibility to plan for is when a husband and wife or heirs die in a common disaster or in close proximity in time. The probabilities of this happening are approximately 1 in 500 if both parties are in their 40's or younger and are in good health. The odds might drop to 1 in 50 or less if both spouses are over 65.[14]

In such rare circumstances, if the assets are held in joint ownership, the Will directs distribution of them. If they are held under a Simple Beneficiary Trust, several beneficiaries can be named. If both spouses are elderly and/or in poor health, co-trustees under a Simple Beneficiary Trust might be chosen rather than joint tenancy.

A problem created by simultaneous death or death in close proximity is illustrated by the following two examples. 1) A couple have children by prior marriages. Each probably prefers their assets go to their respective children and joint ownership will not accomplish this.[15] A clause in their Simple Beneficiary Trust could state that the spouse is the primary beneficiary only if that spouse survives by 7 to 30 days. 2) If the couple has no children, this clause would insure that the assets go to whomever each party chooses.

A requirement that the second spouse survive the first by 180 days before re-registering assets is used by some lawyers in Wills or trusts rather than the shorter period

[14]In our study of 500 probate court cases, we found only one case of a simultaneous death.

[15]A prenuptial agreement and separate Simple Beneficiary Trusts should be made by those with children from prior marriages to insure their assets go to their respective children.

recommended in this book. This 6 month delay might be too long to wait to sell stocks or real estate if good judgement calls for their earlier sale. The usual reason for inserting a time period is to provide protection of assets in cases where both parties die in close proximity, usually as a result of a common accident. Normally problems arise if assets are registered only in each individual's name, and must be probated, taking an average of 16 months.

In Washington, D.C., I studied a case in which assets were left to a Catholic priest by his sister, with an attorney appointed as executor by her Will. The brother died 11 months later with the same attorney as executor under his Will. His sister's assets, which he inherited when she died, were still tied up in probate. This case is an attorney's dream!

The statutes in Washington, D.C. allow the executor to charge 10%. The attorney charged 10% as the executor on those same assets twice. He hired another attorney to handle the legal work. The bottom line is over 30% of the money disappeared in attorneys fees and costs of probate. It might be legal, but is it right? Approximately $35,000 of this money went to the attorneys and costs of probate, and not as the priest intended — to the Church's mental health clinic.

In 326 of the 500 probate court cases studied, information was available as to whether the husband or wife died first. On the average, a wife outlives her husband by seven years and in 70% of the cases studied, the husband died first. For this reason, some people have registered everything in the wife's name, but this will backfire 30% of the time.

Second marriages pose possible problems that can easily be handled by a prenuptial agreement. In the vast majority of states, a husband or wife can elect against a Will or trust and receive 1/3 to 1/2 of your assets regardless of your wishes. A prenuptial agreement is often the only way to handle the situation.

The husband of a very good friend died of cancer when he was only 40. She later remarried and it was her new husband's second marriage also. I told her, "Keep it simple. What is yours is your children's, and what is his is his children's at the death of each of you. Whatever the two of you accumulate after you marry can be worked out like all other couples do." See your attorney to make a prenuptial agreement, and then proceed with the wedding plans.

Chapter 6

WHO GETS IT WHEN YOU GO?

Assets can be left to anyone you wish, with only two exceptions: a spouse cannot be left out completely in most states, and money cannot be left directly to a pet in any state. Other than pets and your spouse, you can leave your assets to anyone you choose by joint tenancy, by holding them under a Simple Beneficiary Trust, or by leaving those assets via a Will. If assets are left by Will, 6% to 22% of your estate is lost to the cost of probate and **not** received by your loved ones.

In most states, spouses who are left nothing can elect against the trust and/or Will and receive what they would be entitled to under that state's laws. Your spouse is generally entitled to 1/3 to 1/2 of your estate, even if you have been separated for years. Divorce any long departed spouse to be sure they do not receive any of your estate.

If a pet is to be provided for, make an agreement with someone to care for the pet. Then leave money to that person, or to a trust on the pet's behalf. Remember, your pet cannot walk into the bank and withdraw money.

In the majority of cases, unhappiness is avoided by leaving everything to one's children equally. If one child has died, then leave his share equally to his children.

Some possible exceptions to the rule of leaving everything to one's children equally: 1) One may be disabled and the others are self-sufficient, 2) You might have a daughter who is divorced with several children to support, and your only other child is a son who is very well off financially.

You can certainly see the wisdom of not leaving funds in the hands of someone incompetent because of mental or emotional problems. In those cases, consider leaving this child's share to a trust with the income to go to him, giving the trustee the authority to spend the principal if the situation requires it.

Never leave money or other assets to a minor directly. Also, never make a minor the beneficiary of a life insurance policy. State laws often require that a guardian be appointed by the court to manage these assets. A surviving spouse is required to be appointed guardian of his/her own children. To avoid court intervention, you can leave assets to your spouse or a trust on behalf of the children.

Let us assume you die without a Will and are survived by a wife, two minor children, and a grandchild (the child of a deceased son). By most states' laws, your assets will be divided as follows:

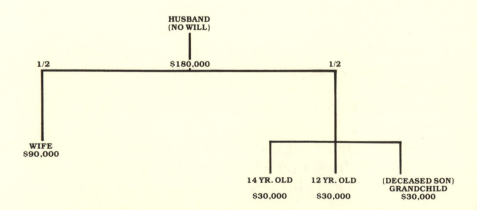

Your wife would receive 1/2 of your assets. Your two children and your grandchild would receive the other 1/2 divided equally.

Let us assume your children are twelve and fourteen years old and your grandchild (the child of a deceased son) is two years old. Three (3) guardianships will be necessary! Your wife will have to go to court and be appointed guardian of each of your two children's assets, and your deceased son's wife will have to be appointed guardian of the assets of your grandchild. This is a legal mess that will take untold hours and money to unsnarl over years of time. This example clearly illustrates the value of having assets held jointly or under a Simple Beneficiary Trust. A Will can also prevent these guardianships if it is properly constructed although it still requires probate proceedings.

A suit for monetary compensation will block the transfer of your assets if left only by Will. Remember, assets in only one name at death will need a court order before they can be transferred to anyone else's name. A suit prevents that court order from being issued, and the assets are effectively frozen. Joint tenancy or a trust is far less frequently contested, and not a single case was found in the 500 files studied. This is reason enough to leave assets by joint tenancy or a trust rather than by Will.

Misfortune can strike any of us. A client of mine discovered two employees had been stealing from him at a furniture store he owned, and they were selling the furniture at a flea market. One of the two was the manager of the store. The owner went to the store with a new manager he had hired, and both were murdered by the two employees. This estate has already been held up for over two years by a wrongful death suit filed by the new manager's widow against those assets in my client's estate that were registered in his name only.

I am sure my client had no idea this was a life threatening situation and was not negligent in his actions. On the other hand, the widow of the new manager no longer has her husband's earnings to support her and her children. Due to the probate court records, the widow and her attorney now know that my client had substantial assets, information otherwise difficult to obtain. The wrongful death suit is withholding distribution of all those assets to his wife, the sole heir.[16]

In this case, it would have been best to re-register the assets under a trust to help minimize federal estate taxes **and** to avoid probate. My client had a Will made just one month before his death that did make some provisions to minimize these taxes and left everything to his wife. It did nothing despite its 18 page length to have his assets avoid probate.

This was a major error made by the attorney who assisted with the estate planning. It resulted in the necessity of probate, and left the assets vulnerable to this unfortunate suit. The Will set up trusts which are called testamentary trusts. If remaining assets ever get out of probate, they can be put in these trusts.

Every state has laws governing distribution of assets for those who die without a Will and have assets registered only in their name. Because these laws can never be right for everyone's individual circumstances, it is up to you to make sure proper measures have been taken so your assets go to the chosen heirs — not to whom the state chooses. Setting up one's assets in joint tenancy or a Simple Beneficiary Trust will do just that. A Will takes care of any miscellaneous assets (such as checks issued only in your name just after your death).

[16]We offer a book on personal injury or wrongful death suits on page 230.

Leaving assets by joint tenancy or a trust will insure the privacy of the financial affairs of your family. Examine the following sample inventory taken from court records. A copy is often sent to everyone named in your Will and is available to anyone who wishes to look at it by going to the probate court office or by sending $1.00 per page for a photostat.

INVENTORY

1. Franklin Savings Bank
   Lex. Ave. & 88th St.
   New York, N.Y.
   ACCT #   6-022450-8 $31,885.71

2. Chemical Bank
   79th St. & York Ave.
   New York, N.Y.
   C.D. #   119-510419   10,000.00

3. American Bell Telephone
   100 shares on deposit with
   Dean Witter Reynolds
   5 World Trade Center
   New York, N. Y.
   ACCT #   661-41340-0-42
   Market Value at Date of Death   4,000.50

4. IBM — 50 shares on deposit
   same account as above
   Value at Date of Death   5,202.00

5. 1983 Mercury Cougar
   Value at Date of Death   6,400.00

TOTAL PROPERTY ON HAND $57,488.21

It becomes a matter of public record if assets are registered in only one name at death. The only state I found in which probate court records are not open to everyone is Delaware. Even there attorneys, beneficiaries named in a Will, and other relatives can examine the file as well as someone doing research as I was. The Register of Wills did have to review all my reasons for wanting to examine the files before granting me access to any records. Obviously more people than you wish could know all about your family's assets.

If I called up your bank and asked for your account balance, they would refuse to give me that information. Sometimes it is difficult to get your own bank balance, much less anyone else's! Not so if assets are registered only in your name at death — then every detail is a matter of public record. **A popular joke among financial planners is that probate court records are an excellent source of new widows with money.**

Chapter 7

JOINT TENANCY

Joint ownership "works" for millions to assure efficient passage of assets at death. In 14 years as a stockbroker, I assisted hundreds in thinking through the appropriateness of joint tenancy for them — with only one problem occurring. One problem in hundreds is better than all these people having their assets embroiled in probate. If a trust or other ways to avoid probate seemed indicated, I explained them.

Assets are owned to a large extent by families — not by just one individual. The family has always been the basic economic unit in any society; joint tenancy is a form of ownership recognizing this and establishes ownership rights of the survivor(s). Often one individual might make most decisions in regard to assets, but the ownership is by two or more individuals.

Since passage of federal legislation in 1976 and 1981, there are very few cases where more federal estate taxes will be owed because of joint ownership. See Chapter 5 again if you need to be refreshed on these changes and assured you will not be subject to these type of taxes. Since passage of this federal legislation, various states are rapidly following suit, but this takes time. I sent a letter to every state's inheritance tax department and spoke to many of their personnel to come up with a quick reference chart for my readers. However, because of differences in how states treat joint ownership, the best solution was a chapter with pointers and a list of questions to ask when calling your state inheritance tax department.

In some states, joint ownership could affect eligibility for homestead exemption. If both joint owners live in the house, the home usually still qualifies. If one joint owner lives elsewhere, the joint owner living in the house might receive only 1/2 the exemption. Check with your county's property tax assessor's office. If this applies to you, then the Simple Trust is probably the best alternative to qualify for homestead exemption and avoid probate.

Another possible drawback for non-spouses who wish to use joint ownership, is the loss of 1/2 the $125,000 exemption from capital gains tax for those over 55 if the second joint owner does not live in the home *or* is not yet 55.

The *only* other possible tax disadvantage to joint ownership is called the "stepped-up basis," and this applies to very few. A brief description follows. For a more in depth discussion if you feel this problem applies to you, see Chapter 5.

The "stepped-up basis" might apply to you as a disadvantage to joint tenancy if you have assets that have appreciated in value. Let us say you have rental property or stocks you bought many years ago at $30,000 now worth $100,000. The capital gains can pass free from income tax if the assets are left by a Simple Trust or by Will rather than joint ownership.

There are three types of joint ownership. I will briefly explain each, and then concentrate on **Joint Tenancy with Right of Survivorship (JTWROS) or JT. TEN.**

JTWROS (or JT. TEN.) — This should appear on the asset(s) similar to the following examples and can be used by any two or more individuals:

Jane B. Smith and

John C. Smith JTWROS
or JT. TEN.

OR

Jane B. Smith and

John C. Smith and

Alan Brown JTWROS
or JT. TEN.

Individuals using this registration do not have to be relatives. Survivors automatically receive any asset registered this way.

Think of a registration under JTWROS as "AND", meaning that each person's signature is necessary to transact business, usually used for real estate and for securities. Bank accounts, commonly referred to as "OR", are Joint Tenancy with Right of Survivorship (**JTWROS or JT. TEN.**), or Tenancy by the Entirety, with a *power-of-attorney built into the signature card*. Read the fine print. This power-of-attorney is what allows one signature to transact business for the account.

JTWROS is often preferred to other registrations because it is widely recognized and understood. If you call your stockbroker and ask to be sent paperwork to change your account to JTWROS, he will automatically know what to do. If you ask that it be changed to Tenancy by the Entirety, he may not understand your request.

Though not permitted in all states, the second type of joint ownership is **Tenancy by the Entirety** (discussed further in Chapter 15). It is primarily used for real estate and can only be used by husband and wife. One possible advantage — it is more difficult for a creditor to attach. A home, which is most people's primary asset, normally cannot be attached by creditors.

A divorce makes assets owned in Tenancy by the Entirety automatically Tenancy in Common, the third type of joint ownership and doomed to probate unless changed.

Always read the forms carefully before opening an account to be sure it will not be **Tenancy in Common**. The following is from an actual application:

> *1.* ***Tenancy in Common****. In the event of the death of either or any of the undersigned, the interests in the tenancy shall be equal unless otherwise specified immediately below. (When a tenant dies, his share is passed by his Will or by state laws if there is no Will, and not to the survivor(s) on the account.)*

> *2.* ***Joint Tenancy with Right of Survivorship****. In the event of the death of either or any of the undersigned, the entire interest in the account shall be vested in the survivor(s).*

Community property and joint tenancy are *not the same.* For those who live in a community property state, the following excerpt from a pamphlet by the Valley National Bank of Arizona might be helpful:

> *"Many people are often confused about the concepts of community property and joint tenancy...community property defines the rights and interests of married persons in property acquired through their labor (during the marriage) in a community property state. Joint tenancy, on the other hand, is a method of titling property which results in the survivor becoming the sole owner."*

Assets registered *only* as community property will not escape probate. Fifty percent (50%) will usually have to go through probate proceedings.*

Any asset registered only with "AND" (without JTWROS or Tenancy by the Entirety after the names) could be presumed Tenancy in Common. There are exceptions: in some states, a deed reading "John C. Smith and Jane B. Smith, husband and wife," is Tenancy by the Entirety, even if these words do not appear on the deed. *The couple, of course, must be husband and wife at the time the deed was made.*

Account agreements you sign at a bank or brokerage firm are accounts in Joint Tenancy with Right of Survivorship or Tenancy by the Entirety. These could be misplaced, or policies of these institutions could change. This is one reason I always made sure "JTWROS" or JT. TEN. appeared after the names on my clients' accounts — eliminating the possibility that it could be construed otherwise.

NOTE: For married couples in some community property states (such as Texas), real property (real estate and securities) does not escape probate, because these assets are jointly held. Consult your realtor and/or stock-broker or attorney, if you live in a community property state as to whether this peculiarity applies in your state. If so, use the living trust. See Chapter 8. Jointly held bank accounts do normally avoid probate even in community property states.

Registrations, with exceptions, must read the following ways in order to avoid probate:

1. Jane B. Smith "OR"
    John C. Smith

2. Jane B. Smith and
    John C. Smith, JOINT TENANCY
    WITH RIGHT OF SURVIVORSHIP

3. Jane B. Smith and
    John C. Smith, JTWROS

4. Jane B. Smith and
    John C. Smith, JT. TEN.
    (stock certificates - brokerage firms
    abbreviation for JTWROS)

5. Jane B. Smith and
    John C. Smith,
    TENANCY BY THE ENTIRETY.
    (Only for husband and wife)

Deeds to property cannot be registered "OR", they must be registered "AND." A deed registered "OR" is invalid. This will be discussed in Chapter 15 on real estate.

An attorney who has written a book on joint ownership claims it is "as bad as drug addiction." He, of course, also does a considerable amount of legal work in probating estates! He blew all out of proportion disadvantages to joint ownership and ignored its numerous advantages. One advantage of joint ownership is that it avoids probate. Joint ownership creates a big disadvantage for attorneys — no thousands in fees!

Let us go over the advantages of JTWROS — there are some excellent ones. First, it avoids probate. By law, the survivor(s) is the owner of the assets as soon as he presents a death certificate and any inheritance tax waivers required. Please be sure to carefully read the disadvantages of joint tenancy at the end of this chapter to be sure you have not missed any negatives to this type of ownership which might be applicable to your situation!

Second, JTWROS is simple to implement. All that is needed is to contact the financial institution involved and get the necessary paperwork signed.

Third, it provides some control over the asset when registered "AND." You might have a child who is over 18, but who you feel cannot manage money. Two signatures would be necessary.

It can be a convenience to sign a power-of-attorney. This makes any asset in "AND" the same as "OR". Each party can then transact business in regard to that asset. It can save thousands in attorney fees if you become incapacitated and helps prevent a guardianship. If you are considering joint ownership and are concerned about a second signature, read Chapter 21 on powers-of-attorney.

As to one of the disadvantages of JTWROS, often cited by attorneys but usually not worth worrying about — the asset can be attached by creditors of the second party on the account. However, if a joint tenant sees possible financial problems ahead, assets can be transferred so future creditors cannot attach them if no fraud is involved.

A very good example of JTWROS took place when my secretary, after typing this chapter, re-registered her brokerage account in JTWROS with her mother. She has access to the money by check or credit card with only one signature as it is a cash management account offered by most brokerage firms. The next day I asked her if she had been up all night worrying about her 70-year-old mother's creditors attaching the account. We both had a good laugh over this.

I am glad to report she also called the bank and requested signature cards to make her checking account "OR", avoiding probate and allowing her mother access to money if the daughter became incapacitated. Just the car is in her name and it is exempt from probate in most states (Chapter 20). She could have also registered the bank account "IN TRUST FOR" on the signature card and signed one of the bank's preprinted powers-of-attorney for her mother. See Chapter 9 on bank accounts.

When single, I owned all my assets in JTWROS with my mother, with my car the exception. This type of registration is often practical for cases of mother and child (over 18), brother and sister, or any others who feel the second party can be relied on to sign and understand that ownership and control of assets is solely yours. The actual owner's name can be first, and his social security number on the asset. This provides more emphasis as to the circumstances surrounding the registration.

Give joint ownership careful consideration. The second party legally owns 1/2 of the asset and can indeed interfere if they so choose. Also, remember the joint tenant has access to your funds and could abscond with them. For a large amount of assets consider a Simple Trust. The more that is involved, the more likely it is there could be differences of opinion by joint owners. If held under a Simple Trust, you have 100% control of the assets and only your signature is needed.

When assets have increased in value or the sum total of the estate will be taxable for federal and/or state inheritance taxes, joint ownership might not be the best alternative for avoiding probate AND minimizing taxes. This applies to a small percentage of readers but if you have any doubt in your mind about the tax status of your estate, re-read Chapter 5. In four states, Maryland, Michigan, Montana, Pennsylvania, inheritance taxes and/or expenses could for some, be less if assets are held jointly. Check with the inheritance department if you live in one of these states and obtain the pamphlet they will send you free of charge.

With joint ownership, two signatures may be required. This is less of a problem with the advent of the new cash management accounts offered by major brokerage firms. Only one signature is necessary to have access to money in the account. Checks and a major credit card are provided.

Only real estate might create an inconvenience when obtaining a second signature.[17] Once I decided to re-register the deed to a condominium in JTWROS with my husband so it would avoid probate. When I mentioned this, he said, "But then you will need my signature if you want to do anything with it." My husband, a wise man, was only trying to protect me from changes life might bring. Then I designed a trust under which to re-register my assets, and so, the Simple Trust evolved.

The use of JTWROS could cause complications for a few people. An example where this is a drawback is where there are children by prior marriages. **If assets are held jointly and one marriage partner dies,** *the survivor legally owns 100% of the assets,* **regardless of the terms of a Will or trust.** The deceased party's children receive nothing which is probably not the way he/she intended.

---

[17]The use of powers-of-attorney to alleviate even this is discussed in Chapter 15 on real estate.

SUMMARY OF THE ADVANTAGES
AND DISADVANTAGES OF *JTWROS:*

ADVANTAGES

1. It avoids probate. The survivor is the owner of the assets. Transfer can take place as soon as a death certificate and necessary inheritance tax waivers are presented.

2. It is easy to implement. All you need do is contact the financial institution involved. They will provide the necessary paperwork. Any attorney can help you re-record a deed. If stock certificates are held individually, any stockbroker can help you obtain new ones.

3. It provides some control over the asset in "AND" as both signatures are necessary. (Be sure the fine print does not say the account or asset is in Tenancy in Common which does not avoid probate.)

4. It can be a convenience to allow someone access to your money when you are incapacitated, in "OR", or in "AND" with a power-of-attorney signed.

5. In a few states, the inheritance tax will be less if assets are held jointly.

6. For a lot of married couples, this type of ownership might be psychologically good for the marriage. This assumes that the assets are under the amount taxed for state inheritance and federal estate taxes. There are only a minor percentage who have to worry about either at the time this book was written.

DISADVANTAGES

1. For non-married joint owners, if the second tenant does not live in a home, you could lose 1/2 your homestead exemption. This occurs in about 1/2 of the states. Call the property tax assessor's office in your county *BEFORE* transferring a deed to a home.

2. For non-married joint owners, again, if your are over 55 and you register your deed in joint ownership, for example, with a child (under 55 or who does not reside in the home), you lose 1/2 of the $125,000 exclusion from capital gains tax when you sell your home!

3. Two signatures can be necessary. This can be solved by a power-of-attorney, by using an "OR" account at the bank, and/or by using one of the new cash management accounts offered by the brokerage firms allowing access to the money with only one signature.

4. With an "AND" account, "control" over the asset could be lost if the second party is not willing to sign.

5. Creditors of the second party can attach the asset. Remember you have legally made the second party a 50% owner of the asset so his creditors can attach "his 50%". Also, in a divorce suit a spouse could try to claim part of this in the property settlement.

6. Assets are not governed by a Will or trust and may by-pass the appropriate heir (See chapter 6).

7. In an "OR" account at the bank and on other assets, the second party could abscond with the money. *For bank accounts, the joint tenant has the freedom to withdraw or write a check for the entire balance and has the right to information regarding the account or asset.* The bank can take money from the account to cover debts owed to it by either party.

8. Problems can arise for assets which have increased in value (capital gain) on a "stepped-up" basis (See Chapter 5).

9. For assets eligible for federal estate and/or state inheritance taxes, joint ownership might not be advisable as it could increase these taxes. (Chapters 5 & 22).

10. If a married couple split up, joint ownership may complicate things.

11. In the event of simultaneous death, the asset would wind up in probate. The probabilities of this occurring are approximately 1 in 500 for a couple in their mid-50's or younger. I prefer joint tenancy for many married couples if their assets are $600,000 or less. In the late 60's or early 70's (earlier if the health of one spouse is poor), I advocate switching to a living trust. Then the legal framework is laid for everything to go smoothly at the death of both spouses.

Chapter 8

SIMPLE BENEFICIARY TRUST

The Simple Beneficiary Trust allows beneficiaries to be designated on all your assets, diamonds to real estate and everything in between. All or part of your assets can be held under a Simple Beneficiary Trust. For example, most of my assets are under a Simple Beneficiary Trust, including the copyright to this book. I also own one piece of property in joint tenancy with my mother. As my situation demonstrates, the Simple Beneficiary Trust will help those who do not feel that joint ownership is sufficient.

Review the following illustration to see why assets registered 1) **only** in your name go to probate 2) while those registered under a trust avoid probate:

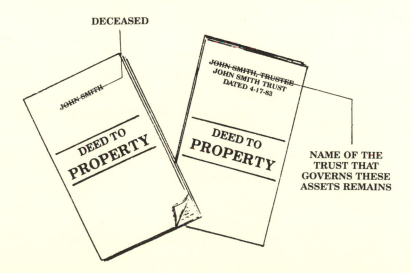

DECEASED

JOHN SMITH

DEED TO PROPERTY

JOHN SMITH, TRUSTEE
JOHN SMITH TRUST
DATED 4-17-83

DEED TO PROPERTY

NAME OF THE TRUST THAT GOVERNS THESE ASSETS REMAINS

The asset registered under a trust, as the part of the illustration depicts, has the description of the trust still remaining on the asset after John Smith's death. The trust provides instructions for distribution.

With a Simple Beneficiary Trust (a living trust), instructions are given in writing while you are living for distribution of your assets at death. Most people believe this is accomplished by a Will, only to have heirs discover they have been led to expensive court proceedings.

Let us say you want to purchase a piece of property, and put it in the name of a corporation. If the deed is registered in your name, instead of the corporation's name, obviously you own the property. A trust, like a corporation, is a separate legal entity. For an asset to be owned and governed by a trust, that asset must be so registered. The reason assets avoid probate with a trust is they are owned by the trust, a legal entity existing beyond your lifetime. Attorneys carefully guard this secret from the public — something so simple that cancels so many fees!

One small disadvantage to a trust is every title, deed, bank and brokerage account must be re-registered under that trust. (A bank account, for example, which was in the name of John C. Smith would now read "John C. Smith, Trustee Under John C. Smith Trust Dated 3-22-83." Or the abbreviated version — "John C. Smith, TTEE John C. Smith U.T.D. 3-22-83"). The minimal work necessary to set up a trust and transfer assets to ownership by the trust will be far less trouble than if those assets wind up in probate as with a Will.

The basic concept of a trust is explained by the following quote from the statutes:

PENNSYLVANIA

WILL SUBSTITUTES, Chapter 7, p. 101

The owner of property may create **substantially the equivalent of a testamentary disposition [Will] through an inter vivos [entered into while you are living]**...such as a trust...it will be recognized as an inter vivos transaction; this is true despite the fact that the owner retains substantial and significant power during his lifetime. Thus, a trust remains valid as an inter vivos one, although the settlor retains . . . the power to revoke or amend, or the power to appoint an interest in the remainder.[18]

Once a Simple Beneficiary Trust is made, it should last a lifetime. The only work involved is the initial few hours to have an attorney draw up a Simple Beneficiary Trust and re-register all assets under it. You will also need to register each new asset under the trust as it is acquired.

Widows or singles will find a Simple Beneficiary Trust is often the best solution to estate planning problems. Some husbands and wives will also find this method advantageous if each has his/her own assets, or when estate or inheritance taxes will be due. Other married couples will often find it practical to have everything in JTWROS.

The IRS has recently ruled that Form 1041 does not need to be filed if the grantor (owner) and trustee are the same. This also means an employer's tax ID number is not required. Take for example, **John C. Smith, Trustee Under John C. Smith Trust Dated 3-22-83**. If your trust is this type, continue to use your Social Security number on assets registered under it. This will be a great boon to popularizing trusts. Previously, it was a real nuisance to keep up with a separate tax ID number, and file additional paperwork with the IRS each year.

[18]Pensylvania Practice, Vol. 1, Probate Law and Taxation of Transfers, Trust and Estates, p. 101.

A trust, unlike a Will, is portable across state lines. When you move, consult an attorney on any changes (rare) that may be required. Often, a Will must be rewritten.

A durable power-of-attorney allows someone to manage your assets if you are incapacitated. However, if you are legally declared incompetent, these proceedings make any power-of-attorney null and void, including a durable one in some states. Where the Uniform Probate Code has passed, the agent you appointed under a durable power-of-attorney may act for you, although he must report to your guardian (Chapter 21 on powers-of-attorney). A power-of-attorney is made null and void by your death and does nothing to help assets avoid probate.

Your successor trustee under a Simple Beneficiary Trust is not hindered from managing your assets and paying for your care if you are declared legally incompetent. Courts only intervene if you are uncooperative, violent, or if the appointed successor trustee mismanages your assets — all rare occurrences.

Do not be disturbed if your attorney's wording is different from trusts contained in this book. If he will not make a trust for you and assist in re-registering your assets, find another attorney. More on how to select an attorney and contract for his services in Chapter 24.

Many prominent people have recognized the advantages of leaving assets by trusts. John Kennedy set up a trust as did Bing Crosby after his first wife's assets went through probate. John Lennon reportedly left $100 to $200 million; his Manhattan court file showed not one single asset had gone through probate. For Arthur Godfrey, who had a "good" Will and whose estate had no complications, there is a file at the same probate court that is close to containing 100 pages. He left $2.5 million. Yet, John Lennon's probate file is only 10 pages. This illustrates the simplicity of leaving assets by trust as opposed to by Will.

Bess Truman's assets have been processed through probate, and all of her last wishes have become public record. I had read about some of these in various publications and purchased a copy of her probate court file through the mail. None of this would have been possible if she had left her assets by trust.

In the study of 500 probate court cases, one was found where all assets had not been re-registered under the trust, but were included on a schedule attached to it. The heirs had to hire an attorney, petition the court, and appear at a hearing before a judge to get a court order to allow the assets to be governed by the trust. This is a very expensive process, which defeats part of the purpose of having a trust — no court proceedings. This is why there is little value to attaching a schedule of assets.

IF THE PAPERWORK WHICH IS PROOF OF OWNERSHIP OF AN ASSET IS NOT RETITLED OR RE-REGISTERED UNDER YOUR TRUST, THE ASSET DOES NOT AVOID PROBATE.

When a trust has been made, assets must be re-registered under it. Write a letter to each institution where you have an account and enclose a copy of the trust for their files. For example:

XYZ Bank
11 Wall Street
New York, N.Y. 10007

Re: Checking Account #600-787-5
     Savings Account #200-782-4

Gentlemen:

Please re-register the two accounts listed above in the following manner:

John C. Smith, Trustee
Under John C. Smith Trust Dated 3-22-83

My address and social security number remain the same. Enclosed is a copy of my Trust for your files.

Please verify by mail or phone (320-4400 during business hours), that this letter has been received. Also place an order for new checks for me.

Please advise me if there is any change in my account number.

Sincerely,

John C. Smith

Bookkeeping for the trust will be the same bookkeeping you have always done. Everything is normally re-registered to ownership by trust and the computer automatically generates account statements in the trust's name proving its existence.

When no money is involved, there is a minimal fee to re-record a deed. A blank quit claim deed can be purchased at a stationery store. Retype the information exactly as it is on the present deed and insert the name of the trust as illustrated in the letter. Have an attorney double check it. You can then re-record the deed at the county courthouse just as efficiently as your attorney's secretary and pay only for his time to double check the accuracy.

A certified copy of your trust is one with your actual signature notarized and witnessed, or a copy certified by an authority (officer of a brokerage firm or the recorder of documents at your county courthouse). Make sure one is always available for real estate transfers and/or for stock certificates (when not kept on deposit with the broker). Be safe, keep an original in your safe deposit box **and record a copy with the recorder of documents**. Do not hesitate to record a trust as you would a deed. If keeping your assets confidential is of importance remember — courthouses have endless recorded documents and no one bothers to read them. If you want to take precautions to insure confidentiality, there is a method. On the schedule of assets sheet (attached to your trust), write $1.00 (only). Then all that is revealed is who you have left your assets to and not how much. Attorneys who object to filing a trust with the recorder of documents for the sake of confidentiality forget that if assets go through probate every detail including bank acccount numbers will be accessible to any interested party.

In a sad case studied, the Will was destroyed in a house fire that also killed the husband and wife. The court permitted the copy from their attorneys files to be used, but a hearing had to be held which required the witnesses of the Will to attend. It was expensive and inconvenient to the witnesses and family.

Stock transfer agents require a certified copy of the trust for each stock certificate **not** placed on deposit with a brokerage firm. Agents accept copies that your brokerage firm guarantees are from a certified copy (signature notarized and properly witnessed).

A copy of the trust is on file with the brokerage firm where stocks have been placed on deposit as was required when they were re-registered under the trust. When stocks of several companies are on deposit, a certified copy of the trust is not needed for each stock at death. Only a copy of the death certificate is necessary. Other financial institutions do not require a copy of the trust at death because a certified copy was provided when the assets were transferred into the name of the trust. A certified copy of the trust will be required when real estate is sold or transferred to your heirs.

DO NOT BE MISLEAD INTO A "TESTAMENTARY TRUST," ONE ESTABLISHED UNDER YOUR WILL. ANY ASSETS **ONLY IN YOUR NAME** MUST GO THROUGH PROBATE BEFORE THEY CAN BE PUT IN SUCH A TRUST. SEE PAGE 33.

In most states, a trust is irrevocable if not specified as **revocable** in the agreement. This provision could easily be omitted in the typing. This is less likely for an attorney to overlook.

Creditors can attach the assets of the trust in some cases but the assets are completely protected from attachment by the creditors of the beneficiaries at your death or any other parties when the proper clause is included (See item 6. Creditors, in this Chapter.)

To revoke your Simple Beneficiary Trust, a sample format is provided in Appendix V. Usually, you would make a new Simple Beneficiary Trust that revokes previous ones, providing it contains a paragraph to that effect. Small changes to your Simple Beneficiary Trust can be made by an amendment.

This trust agreement is lengthy but remember it must cope with all the problems life brings and a changing world. If for any reason the one drawn for you is defective in its construction or wording, remember it can be completely revoked! See No. 5 of this sample trust.

NOTE: Since you are going to an attorney for help with the final details of your estate planning (Trust and/or Will), you might wish to discuss with him executing a Living Will. This would provide your family with all the ammunition possible to see that your life was not unnecessarily prolonged if your condition were hopeless or terminal. If you wish further information on the Living Will, write Concern for Dying, Suite 831, 250 W. 57th St., New York, N.Y. 10107, 1-212-246-6962. A nonprofit organization.

Format of a trust as an example. (It is assumed all children who are beneficiaries of this trust are over 18. If under 18, or you do not want them to receive assets until age 25, 30, or 35, discuss with your attorney how to handle via the same basic format as follows):

SIMPLE BENEFICIARY TRUST

TRUST AGREEMENT
of
Jane B. Smith

I, Jane B. Smith, a resident of Baltimore County, Maryland and being of sound mind, make this Trust Agreement of my own free will and revoke any other Trust Agreements I previously executed, and any amendments to these prior Trust Agreements. I, Jane B. Smith, designate myself as Trustee.

1. Trust Purpose: The purpose of this Trust is to hold all assets owned by this Trust for the benefit of the children of Jane B. Smith. If one child is deceased or unwilling to receive his/her share, that child's children are to share equally in that child's share. At the time this Trust Agreement was executed, Jane B. Smith had four children. Jane B. Smith's son, John C. Smith, Jr., is to receive her car(s). Her silver, china, and crystal go to her daughter, Linda Smith Johnson. Distribution of Jane B. Smith's other personal possessions or the above if the beneficiary is deceased or unwilling to receive them, is left to the sole discretion of the Successor Trustee.

Jane B. Smith may use any of the principal and income from the Trust's assets for her own support, general welfare, education, and health for as long as she lives at her sole discretion. If she should become incapacitated as defined, a Successor Trustee is named. At the death of Jane B. Smith, any named Successor Trustee shall transfer assets, and income from them, to the beneficiaries and this Trust terminates.

2. <u>Trust Name and Property</u>: This Trust shall be known as the Jane B. Smith Trust Dated November 17, 1983. All property registered as "Jane B. Smith Trustee, Under Jane B. Smith Trust Dated 11-17-83" or an abbreviated version of this shall be governed by this Trust Agreement. The Grantor (Owner) and Trustee, Jane B. Smith, has executed all the instructions separately in writing to transfer and deliver to the Trustee all her assets to be held by this Trust according to the terms and conditions as specified herein.

3. <u>Successor Trustee</u>: If Jane B. Smith is incapacitated as certified in writing by two licensed physicians or is deceased, the Successor Trustee shall be John C. Smith, Jr., her son. If he is deceased or unable or unwilling to serve, then Linda Smith Johnson, her daughter, shall be the Successor Trustee. The Successor Trustee agrees to serve with no compensation unless it is agreed to by all the beneficiaries.

The Trustee or any Successor Trustee may expend income and/or principal of the assets owned by this Trust to provide for the health, education, support and general welfare of Jane B. Smith in the manner of living to which she is accustomed. The Successor Trustee may also add to income and/or principal, or make changes in the investments of this Trust at his/her sole and absolute discretion.

If Jane B. Smith is incapacitated as certified in writing by two licensed physicians, her Successor Trustee may, on her behalf, employ or terminate physicians, nurses, nursing homes, hospital and others at his/her sole discretion for Jane B. Smith's care. Any Successor Trustee may sign instructions and consents as required by an attending physician, hospital or nursing home, etc.

4. <u>Management</u>: Jane B. Smith, the Trustee, or any Successor Trustee shall have all the powers Jane B. Smith would have if she were acting as a legally competent individual. Management of the assets owned by this Trust shall be at the Trustee's or Successor Trustee's sole discretion. This includes the right to borrow against or pledge any of the assets, including the right to mortgage real estate or margin stocks.

5. <u>Right to Revoke or Change</u>: Jane B. Smith reserves the right to revoke, amend or make changes to this Trust Agreement at any point during her lifetime.

6. <u>Creditors</u>: The assets owned by this Trust are not accessible in any way by creditors of her beneficiaries, Successor Trustee or their past or present spouses.

7. <u>Bond and Accounting</u>: No bond shall be required of the Trustee or any Successor Trustee. The Trustee or any Successor Trustee may do any accounting of the Trust's assets to the sole discretion of any Successor Trustee, and need not comply with the provisions of the trust accounting statutes of Maryland as they presently exist or may be amended, or any new statutes in this regard.*

8. <u>Taxes & Debts</u>: The Successor Trustee can pay from assets of the Trust debts and taxes of Jane B. Smith as he/she deems proper and reasonable.

9. <u>Disappearance</u>: If Jane B. Smith should disappear, the Successor Trustee shall manage the assets as provided by this Trust. If she is not heard from for two years, and her body is not recovered, all the assets are to be distributed as provided in this Trust Agreement.

*Optional: When there are several beneficiaries, you could request that your Sucessor Trustee have a tax advisor send them accounting statements specifying amounts and the source.

This Trust Agreement was executed in triplicate in Maryland and shall be enforced under the laws of that state. Any copies signed and executed by Jane B. Smith shall be treated the same as an original.

_____

Jane B. Smith

We witnessed Jane B. Smith sign this Trust Agreement in triplicate on 17 November 1983, and witnessed each others signatures at her request. We also attest that she appeared to be of sound mind and to sign this Trust Agreement of her own free will.

Witness: _____   Witness: _____

Address: _____   Address: _____

_____   _____
City   State   City   State

STATE OF MARYLAND
COUNTY OF _____

Notary: Jane B. Smith, who appeared before me and who was duly sworn, signed this Trust Agreement. She stated she did so of her own free will and appeared to be of sound mind.

       WITNESS my hand and official seal, this _____day of _____A.D. 19_____.

                              _____
                              Signature Notary
                              State of Maryland at Large

My commission expires _____

Chapter 9

BANK AND SAVINGS & LOAN LEAGUE ACCOUNTS

At every bank and savings and loan association in the nation, an "OR" account (either party can transact business for the account) can be established to avoid probate.

On an IRA (Individual Retirement Account) or Keogh (retirement plan for self employed), which must be in one name, the bank allows a primary and contingent beneficiary to be designated, again avoiding probate.

In the fine print, an "OR" account, as it is commonly referred to, is Joint Tenancy with Right of Survivorship, or sometimes with married couples, Tenancy by the Entirety. What makes it "OR" is the power-of-attorney built into the account agreement.

At all banks visited, I was assured the survivor on an "OR" account would receive the money on presentation of a death certificate. If "OR" appears between the names, survivors' rights are self-explanatory and need no further documentation. Many assets can be held in "OR," such as bank accounts, credit union accounts, Series E and H

bonds, U.S. Treasury Bills and other government securities, automatically going to survivors. Asset management
accounts at brokerage firms are the equivalent of "OR" but
brokerage accounts, individually held stock certificates
and real estate must be "AND". See Chapter 15 for an explanation as why.

Any account which reads either of the following ways
could be assumed to be Tenancy in Common and be sen-
tenced to probate:

1. John C. Smith
   Jane B. Smith

2. John C. Smith and
   Jane B. Smith

If 1) "OR" 2) JTWROS (Joint Tenancy with Right of
Survivorship) or 3) Tenancy by the Entirety does not appear after the names, off to probate those assets could go.
Note, the two above examples do not have any of these
three after the names. The exception to this is if the bank
or brokerage house account agreements list some type of
survivorship rights. Because agreements can be misplaced over the years, I strongly recommend one of these
registrations be printed on account statements.

Disadvantages of "OR" accounts are the same as joint
ownership, but with more force. Banks generally make
both parties liable for bad checks drawn on accounts. In
many cases, the bank can take money for any debts at that
bank not paid by either party. You should absolutely trust
anyone you plan to enter a joint tenancy agreement with.
If you do not, then the Simple Beneficiary Trust is for you,
or hold the account "IN TRUST FOR", explained further in
this chapter.

There are five possible ways to keep bank accounts out

of probate. Of the 500 cases studied, 68% had bank accounts end up in probate, a senseless loss of money (6% to 22%). It is easy for bank accounts to avoid probate. Five ways follow:

1) In "OR" accounts as we have already discussed.

2) In "AND" — either JTWROS or Tenancy by the Entirety. No power-of-attorney is built into the signature card, two signatures are required. (Read the fine print to make sure it is not Tenancy in Common which must go through probate.)

3) "IN TRUST FOR" without a trust agreement of your own; the **trust agreement is usually on the card you sign or banks feel this phrase alone is sufficient**. Most banks will do this. If your bank does not, go to the Yellow Pages under Banks and call several - you will find one who will. Such an account reads one of the following ways:

John C. Smith **IN TRUST FOR** Jane B. Smith

or

ABBREVIATED

John C. Smith **I.T.F.** Jane B. Smith

or

Jane B. or John C. Smith **I.T.F. (IN TRUST FOR)** Linda Smith Johnson

4) Under a Simple Beneficiary Trust or other trust agreement. The account would read one of the following ways:

John C. Smith **TRUSTEE,**
UNDER John C. Smith **TRUST**
DATED 4-17-83

or

ABBREVIATED

John C. Smith,**TTEE**
John C. Smith **U.T.D. 4-17-83**

5) By designating a beneficiary on bank accounts in 14 states which have passed the Uniform Probate Code. It is often referred to as **Payment-on-Death (P.O.D)**. The 14 states are Alaska, Arizona, Colorado, Idaho, Maine, Michigan, Minnesota, Montana, Nebraska, New Jersey, New Mexico, North Dakota, Pennsylvania, and Utah.

As already mentioned, banks will also hold an account **"IN TRUST FOR" without you providing them a trust agreement**. This type of account **allows you to designate a beneficiary**. Most banks will allow you to do this. Another word of warning — never hold an account "IN TRUST FOR" a minor because there is no separately drawn trust agreement that appoints a successor trustee to manage the money for the minor. At your death, the bank account goes directly to the minor, probably necessitating an adult being the court appointed guardian, or at best, severely restricting use of the money.

Reminder — do not make a minor the beneficiary of a bank account or life insurance policy. They have no legal right to make contracts. In the eyes of the law, they are babies and a court appointed guardian will usually be necessary. This is discussed further in Chapter 23 for people with minor children.

"IN TRUST FOR" is referred to as a Totten Trust and so named because Totten was the first person to use this type of registration. Some banks will not use this for checking accounts, so use the phone to shop for one that will allow you to use it if you feel this is the most desirable arrangement for you. Another alternative to consider is adding someone else's name on a joint account with the use of "OR."

Bank accounts held in joint tenancy are often frozen at the death of either tenant in states with inheritance taxes. However, accounts held in any type of trust, such as the Simple Beneficiary Trust or "IN TRUST FOR," sometimes are not frozen. Check with your state inheritance tax department on this point.

If you think the use of "IN TRUST FOR" is appropriate for you in avoiding probate, read this section. We have talked with numerous banks in different states. Most will let you hold an "IN TRUST FOR" account for more than one person. If you have two children to share the account equally, the account could read:

Jane B. Smith IN TRUST FOR
John C. Smith, Jr. AND Linda Smith Johnson

One bank advised this type of account should read "OR" instead of the "AND" underlined. I would not advise "OR" since one child could take all the money. Bank employees are in the habit of advising "OR" since much of their day to day business is dependent on signatures. A check is far less likely to cause a problem to the person writing it, or the bank, when only one signature is necessary. However, only death necessitates these two signatures.

The bank's computer allows two or three lines (usually 32 characters each) for designating accounts. Insist that the name the account is "IN TRUST FOR" appears on your computer statements (not necessarily your checks) be-cause if account cards are lost or misplaced, the bank ac-count may not avoid probate. There would be nothing to prove it was "IN TRUST FOR" if it was not printed on your account statements.

In theory, an "IN TRUST FOR" account can be held for four or five people (exceeding the spaces on any computer) by using the account agreement. If you attempt this, you will probably try the patience of some bank employees. Be persistent, most will do it.

At many savings & loan associations, designations for "IN TRUST FOR", CO-TRUSTEES, and as many as three beneficiaries can be made on the signature card.

Hint — keep your name the same on all legal docu-ments. Several times I had clients who purchased stock over a period of years, and the name differed on the various certificates. An officer of my firm had to sign an affidavit that the person was one and the same. This is a minor problem compared to probate.

In states with inheritance tax, bank accounts are fro-zen at death, so spouses often have accounts in each name alone to make sure funds will be free at death for the sur-vivor. This is all right if these accounts were held "IN TRUST FOR" or if a beneficiary was designated on the account to avoid probate (allowed only in the 14 states that have passed the Uniform Probate Code).

Every state has provisions to free some of the money to the survivors if accounts are frozen. For example, in South Carolina, $10,000 may be drawn out of a bank account al-though funds over this amount are frozen. In New Jersey 50% of the funds are frozen but this allows use of the other 50% by the survivor(s). **Most fears that survivors will be penniless because of the inheritance tax department are**

unfounded. It is assets stuck in probate that heirs should fear!

To be sure everybody understands; joint accounts with the use of "OR" cannot be left to your heirs by Will. By law, this type of account belongs to the surviving joint owner.

An example that illustrates this clearly — while I waited to get some answers at the probate court in Manhattan, I overheard a man talking to the clerk. His sister had everything in joint accounts with him when she died, yet her money was left to three people in her Will. The brother was asking the clerk to have the probate court distribute assets already legally his as the survivor. I could see he was perplexed! He could distribute them voluntarily as per the Will, but there were questions in his mind as to his sister's true intent. What had she really wanted?

To summarize, the five ways to set up bank accounts to avoid probate are as follows:

1. "OR" - which is really JTWROS or Tenancy by the Entirety with power-of-attorney built into the card or agreement you sign. Disadvantages peculiar to "OR" bank accounts:

a. The second party has the freedom to withdraw money or write a check for the entire balance in the account.

b. The bank can take money out of the account to cover debts owed to that bank by either party.

c. The second party has a right to information about the account. Remember, he is legally a co-owner of the account. This is usually not a disadvantage since most people respect your privacy.

2. "AND" such as in Joint Tenancy with Right of Survivorship or Tenancy by the Entirety (the same thing, but for husband and wife only). These accounts require both signatures. Read the fine print to make **sure the account is not Tenancy in Common**.

3. Using the bank's signature cards without your own trust agreement. It should read as follows: Jane B. Smith I.T.F. (IN TRUST FOR) John C. Smith.

4. Your own trust agreement (such as a Simple Beneficiary Trust) reading "Jane B. Smith, Trustee Under Jane B. Smith Trust Dated 11-17-83," or as popularly abbreviated "Jane B. Smith, TTEE Jane B. Smith U.T.D. 11-17-83."

5. You can designate one or more beneficiaries to receive the proceeds in an account in 14 states that have adopted the Uniform Probate Code. It is called Payment-on-Death (P.O.D.). The 14 states are Alaska, Arizona, Colorado, Idaho, Maine, Michigan, Minnesota, Montana, Nebraska, New Jersey, New Mexico, North Dakota, Pennsylvania, and Utah.

Chapter 10

COPYRIGHTS/PATENTS/ROYALTIES

A patent, copyright, or royalty contract must be applied for by an individual, by coauthors or coinventors, or by the corporation or company that employs them. Ownership of these can be held in joint ownership or under a trust.

An actual copyright application follows illustrating how to **transfer ownership** at the time you **apply** for a copyright.

4

See instructions before completing this space.

COPYRIGHT CLAIMANT(S) Name and address must be given even if the claimant is the same as the author given in space 2.▼

Barbara R. Stock
1950 Lee Rd.,Suite 214
Winter Park, Fl. 32789

TRANSFER If the claimant(s) named here in space 4 are different from the author(s) named in space 2, give a brief statement of how the claimant(s) obtained ownership of the copyright.▼
Barbara R. Stock, Trustee, Under Barbara R. Stock Trust Dated 12-29-83

It usually takes several months before one receives the copyright registration number, or in the case of a patent, perhaps years before the number is received. If the registration number is available, list it in the trust agreement or Simple Beneficiary Trust.

If a copyright has already been granted and paperwork needs to be done to transfer ownership to joint ownership or a trust, call the FORMS HOTLINE 1-202-287-9100, and order Circular R12, <u>Recordation of Transfers and Other Documents</u>.

To transfer ownership of a patent, call the patent office 1-202-557-3158 or write — Superintendent of Documents, Government Printing Office, Washington, D.C. 20402 — and request they send you <u>General Information Concerning Patents</u> (booklet is free). In most cases you can complete the copyright paperwork yourself. Assistance from an attorney specializing in this area is probably necessary for a patent. You will need less of an attorney's expensive time if you know what is to be done and can check the accuracy of it.

The only thing necessary to re-register a patent, copyright, or royalty at your death is a letter of instruction from your successor trustee, a copy of your trust, and a copy of your death certificate.

You might want to hold a patent, copyright, or royalty in a trust separate from your Simple Beneficiary Trust. This allows the benefits of the copyright or patent to continue for many years while the remainder of the estate is settled. Duration of a patent is 17 years, a copyright is the author's lifetime, **plus** 50 years, and a royalty as per the contract. Whether the copyright or patent is held under a Simple Beneficiary Trust or a separate trust, someone is designated to negotiate on behalf of beneficiaries. Here is a sample trust:

TRUST AGREEMENT

for

Copyrights

of

Jane B. Smith

I, Jane B. Smith, a resident of Wilson County, North Carolina and being of sound mind, make this Trust Agreement of my own free will and revoke any other Trust Agreements for Copyrights I previously executed, and any amendments to these prior Trust Agreements for Copyrights.

1. <u>Trust Purpose</u>: Jane B. Smith holds any copyrights owned by this Trust for the benefit of her husband, John C. Smith. If he is not living, then her parents, Ruth D. Brown and/or James E. Brown are the beneficiaries to the copyright(s) owned by this Trust. Jane B. Smith shall receive all benefits or income from any copyrights owned by this Trust for as long as she lives and the use of any proceeds as she sees fit. A Successor Trustee is named in the event Jane B. Smith is incapacitated as defined. At the death of Jane B. Smith, the Successor Trustee shall distribute all the assets and any income from them owned by this Trust as per above and this Trust terminates.

2. <u>Trust Name and Property</u>: This Trust shall be known as the "Jane B. Smith Trust for Copyrights Dated 12-18-83." Jane B. Smith, the Grantor (Owner), transfers to the Trustee, Jane B. Smith, the ownership of Copyright Number 0262435, <u>How to Paint Walls</u>. Instructions have been sent to the copyright office to re-record and transfer ownership to "Jane B. Smith, Trustee Under Jane B. Smith Trust for Copyrights Dated 12-18-83."

3. <u>Successor Trustee</u>: If Jane B. Smith is incapacitated as certified in writing by two licensed physicians or is deceased, John C. Smith shall be the Successor Trustee. If he is deceased or unable or unwilling to serve, Ruth D. Brown shall be the Successor Trustee. The Successor Trustee agrees to serve at no compensation unless it is agreed to by all beneficiaries.

4. <u>Management</u>: Jane B. Smith, the Trustee, or any Successor Trustee shall have sole discretion as to the management, income, and benefits from the copyright(s) and the privilege to borrow against or pledge it as collateral. Also, to negotiate and enter into any contracts for the copyright.

5. <u>Right to Revoke or Change</u>: Jane B. Smith reserves the right to revoke, amend or make changes to this Trust at any point during her lifetime.

6. <u>Creditors</u>: The assets owned by this Trust are not accessible in any way by creditors of her beneficiaries, Successor Trustee or their past or present spouses.

7. <u>Bond and Accounting</u>: No bond or accounting shall be required of the Trustee or any Successor Trustee.

8. <u>Debts and Taxes</u>: The Successor Trustee can pay from assets of the Trust any debts or taxes of Jane B. Smith he/she deems proper and reasonable.

9. <u>Disappearance</u>: Jane B. Smith and/or any subsequent beneficiary shall be presumed dead if after two years she has not been heard from and the body is not recovered. All assets and income owned by this Trust may then be distributed. The Successor Trustee can manage assets as provided in this Trust during that two year period.

10. This Trust Agreement for Copyrights is executed in triplicate in North Carolina and shall be enforced under the laws of that state. Any copies signed and executed by Jane B. Smith will be treated the same as originals.

_____

Jane B. Smith

Witness: _____   Witness: _____

Address: _____   Address: _____

| City | State | City | State |

STATE OF NORTH CAROLINA
COUNTY OF _____

NOTARY: Jane B. Smith, who appeared before me and was duly sworn, signed this Trust Agreement. She stated she did so of her own free will and appeared to be of sound mind.

WITNESS my hand and official seal, this _____day
of _____A.D. 19_____.

_____
Signature Notary
State of North Carolina at Large

My commission expires _____

Schedule of Assets

Copyright # 0262435 on How to Paint Walls

Author, Jane B. Smith

(The real necessity is to be sure the Copyright office shows
the Copyright owned by your trust — it does perform a legal technicality to list something when the trust is executed on the schedule although I see no point of keeping
the schedule up to date — **if all copyrights and applica-
tions for copyrights are registered in the name of the
trust.**)

Chapter 11

CORPORATIONS

Small corporations as well as large ones issue stock certificates to represent ownership. These certificates can be "registered" in joint tenancy, or under a trust. If you are the sole owner on a stock certificate of any **size** corporation, it will go straight to probate court.

A corporation is a separate entity owned by its stockholders. This is true even if there is only one stockholder.

Since stock certificates are the equivalent of a deed to a home or title to a car, the proof of ownership, they should be registered in one of the following ways:

John C. Smith and
Jane B. Smith, **Joint
Tenancy with Right
of Survivorship**

or

John C. Smith and
Jane B. Smith, **Tenancy
by the Entirety**
(only for husband and wife)

or

John C. Smith, Trustee Under
John C. Smith Trust Dated 4-12-83
Or the Abbreviated Version
John C. Smith, **TTEE**
John C. Smith, **U.T.D., 4-12-83**

Jointly owned stock certificates **cannot** be registered in "**OR**." A stock power can in essence make it "**OR**," but stock certificates are not, as a rule, legally valid if the word "**OR**" instead of "**AND**" is printed between the names. See Chapter 15 for why this holds true for deeds to property also. See Chapter 19 for a discussion on stock powers.

Transfer of the stock certificate should be entered on the ledger for stock transfers. It takes only a few minutes to type information on a stock certificate, and record it on the stock transfer ledger. If you do not have a corporate kit, purchase one at a stationery store.

Chapter 12

CREDIT UNION ACCOUNTS

There are two ways to avoid probate for credit union accounts:

1) In "**OR**" just as at a bank. This is simply **JTWROS** with the power-of-attorney built into the signature card.

2) Designate a beneficiary(ies) by cards provided by the credit union. This is allowed by every single credit union we have contacted.*

In the five hundred cases studied, the number of credit union accounts in probate was less than 4%, as opposed to 68% for bank accounts. **What works is what counts**. The ability to designate beneficiaries evidently helps keep these accounts out of our probate courts. The very few probated might have been due to the death of beneficiaries.

---

*A trust is not accepted at Federal Credit Unions although some state credit unions might take trust agreements. The reason is that they do business with "natural persons" (individuals). A trust or a corporation are separate legal entities and not "natural persons".

Below is a copy of the card credit unions use to designate a beneficiary to money in an account. Another beneficiary can be designated to the maximum $2,000 automatic free life insurance on a share (savings) account.* A card is provided for each.

Account Number   Date

_____

Designation of Beneficiary (Beneficiaries) for

PAYABLE-UPON-DEATH ACCOUNT

The undersigned, Settlor, a member of the _____
_____Credit Union, hereby **establishes this account** and places the funds in said account **in trust for the following beneficiary**(beneficiaries):

_____   _____
Name   Address

*Advantages and disadvantages of "**OR**" accounts are explained in Chapter 9.

Name	Address

This account shall be held in trust by Settlor to control and dispose of as he sees fit and shall be otherwise freely revocable by Settlor, said revocation to take effect only upon notice in writing to this Credit Union. Upon Settlor's death, the full amount then standing to the credit of this account shall be payable to the Beneficiary or equally to the beneficiaries. The above credit union shall be exempt from all liability for payment to Beneficiary of any sums from this account upon proof of Settlor's death.

Witness	Signature of Settlor

The above is also a trust agreement if you read the card carefully. Once you understand the legal fine points of trusts, you will see they are instruments allowing you to designate beneficiaries to any and all assets.

Here is the card for designating both a primary and contingent beneficiary. The previous card was only for primary beneficiary(ies).

Account Number   Date

Designation of Principal & Contingent Beneficiaries for

PAYABLE-UPON-DEATH ACCOUNT

The undersigned, Settlor, a member of the _____
_____Credit Union, hereby **establishes
this account** and places the funds in said account **in Trust
for the following beneficiary**(beneficiaries):

Principal Beneficiary

_____   _____
            Name   Address

Contingent Beneficiary

_____   _____
            Name   Address

**This account shall be held in trust by Settlor to control
and dispose of as he sees fit** and shall be otherwise freely
revocable by Settlor, said revocation to take effect only
upon notice in writing to this Credit Union. Upon Settlor's
death, the full amount then standing to the credit of this
account shall be payable to the Principal Beneficiary if living, otherwise to the Contingent Beneficiary. The above
credit union shall be exempt from all liability for payment
to Beneficiary of any sums from this account upon proof
of Settlor's death.

_____   _____
           Witness   Signature of Settlor

Chapter 13

JEWELRY, ANTIQUES, LIVESTOCK AND OTHER MISCELLANEOUS ITEMS

Everyone owns numerous items that have no actual piece of paper or title that is proof of ownership. In most states, these items will pass to one's spouse exempt from probate, especially the contents of a home held in joint ownership. These items might be subject to state inheritance tax. Taxes and probate are **separate** problems which must be resolved.

Other than spouses, clarify to whom you wish items to go to under a trust. For example, you are widowed and wish to leave everything to your children. All these items, no matter how valuable, from diamond rings to clothing, can avoid probate by being mentioned in your Simple Beneficiary Trust (or by the use of a separate trust). Even if you do not have any highly valuable items, but have more than one beneficiary, it might be wise to clarify in writing who you want to receive various items. The following is an example of a paragraph to include in a Simple Beneficiary Trust:

> *"Her diamond wristwatch is to be given to her mother. Her china and crystal are to go to her daughter, Linda Smith Johnson. All other personal effects and belongings shall be distributed and/or sold at the sole and absolute discretion of her Successor Trustee."*

Please be sure the terminology expresses possession by using "my" or "his/her." Then the successor trustee will not be confused as to whether this item is to be purchased for a beneficiary if the item had been lost, sold, or stolen prior to your death.

Here is another example. A widowed mother and spinster daughter might have lived together for years. The mother might not have anything of great value, but her wish is for all household items and clothing to go to this daughter even though she might have other children. Mentioning this in her Simple Beneficiary Trust would insure there was no misunderstanding.

Another example might be — a widow has only one child, and owns all her assets jointly with that child. A trust agreement could be drawn up to cover only miscellaneous personal belongings. This might not be necessary if you think no one will object. The child could just take possession of these items.

If there are numerous items of substantial value, you may want to register them under a separate trust, minimizing the length of your Simple Beneficiary Trust. This would avoid disclosing personal details to your financial institutions since a copy of the trust must be provided for them. A notarized copy of only the portion of the trust agreement that applies to management of assets and the designation of the trustee and successor trustee could be provided in lieu of the entire document.

If you think it might be necessary, describe personal possessions, where they are normally kept, and even include a picture in your trust if you think it is needed. A sample of a separate trust is provided here for those who might own all other assets jointly or for those who wish to separate these items from their Simple Beneficiary Trust. If there are numerous items requiring several pages, you might want to make a separate trust so as to minimize the length of your Simple Beneficiary Trust.

The following is a sample trust format for educational purposes:

TRUST AGREEMENT

for

Personal Property

of

Jane B. Smith

I, Jane B. Smith, a resident of Bell County, Texas and being of sound mind, make this Trust Agreement and revoke any Trust Agreements for Personal Property I previously executed, and any amendments to these prior Trust Agreements for Personal Property.

1. Trust Purpose: Jane B. Smith holds in trust all the assets owned by this trust for the benefit of the beneficiaries as enumerated under 3. Beneficiaries. Jane B. Smith, the trustee, reserves the right to sell and use the proceeds, insure, or borrow against any and all assets owned by this trust during her lifetime.

At the death of Jane B. Smith, any named Successor Trustee shall transfer assets and income from them to beneficiaries of this Trust and this Trust terminates.

2. Trust Name and Trust Property: This Trust shall be known as the "Jane B. Smith Trust Dated 11-21-83 for Personal Property" or an abbreviated version of this.

Jane B. Smith is both Grantor (Owner) and Trustee. Jane B. Smith does hereby transfer to ownership of this Trust the following items:

a.) Her diamond wristwatch which she normally wears.

b.) Her pair of gold and diamond earrings kept in her jewelry box; gold hoops with one small row of diamonds on each side with a total carat weight of .83, for pierced ears.

c.) Her china, eight place settings with serving pieces, the pattern is Lacepoint by Lennox, kept in her home in the kitchen cabinets.

d.) Her solid sterling silver, eight place settings with serving pieces, of Damask Rose by Oneida. The sterling is in Jane B. Smith's silver chest usually on the credenza in her dining room.

e.) All other personal possessions, clothing, and household furnishings she might own at her death.

3. <u>Beneficiaries</u>: The items enumerated under trust property shall be designated to beneficiaries as follows: a) Diamond wristwatch — her daughter, Linda Smith Johnson. If she is deceased or unable or unwilling to receive it, then her granddaughter, Margaret Johnson. b.) The gold and diamond hoop earrings — her granddaughter, Margaret Johnson. If she is deceased or unable or unwilling to receive them, then her granddaughter, Helen Johnson Richards. c.) The china, Lacepoint by Lennox — her granddaughter, Helen Johnson Richards. If she is deceased or unable or unwilling to receive it, then her grandson, Robert A. Johnson. d.) The sterling silver, Damask Rose by Oneida — her grandson, Robert A. Johnson. If he is deceased or unable or unwilling to receive it, then her granddaughter, Helen Johnson Richards. e) All other personal possessions, clothing, household furnishings and

any of the items a through d, if the beneficiaries are deceased or unable or unwilling to receive them shall be distributed and/or sold at the sole and absolute discretion of her Successor Trustee.

4. <u>Successor Trustee</u>: If Jane B. Smith is incapacitated as verified in writing by two licensed physicians or is deceased, the Successor Trustee shall be Linda Smith Johnson her daughter. If Linda Smith Johnson is deceased or unable or unwilling to serve, then her granddaughter, Margaret Johnson, is requested to be Successor Trustee. At Jane B. Smith's death, any Successor Trustee shall distribute assets owned by this Trust and this Trust terminates. The Successor Trustee agrees to serve with no compensation unless it is agreed to by all the beneficiaries.

5. <u>Management</u>: Jane B. Smith, Trustee or any Successor Trustee shall have all powers that Jane B. Smith would have if she were acting as a legally competent individual, and still owned all of the assets of the Trust only in her name. This includes the right to change any insurance and borrow against or pledge these assets.

6. <u>Right to Revoke or Change</u>: Jane B. Smith reserves the right to revoke, amend or change this Trust Agreement at any point during her lifetime.

7. <u>Creditors</u>: The assets owned by this Trust are not accessible in any way by creditors of her beneficiaries, Successor Trustee, or any of their past or present spouses.

8. <u>Bond and Accounting</u>: No bond or accounting shall be required of Jane B. Smith, Trustee, or any Successor Trustee. The Trustee or any Successor Trustee may do any accounting of the Trust's assets at her sole discretion and she need not comply with the provisions of the Trust accounting statutes of Texas as they presently exist or may be amended, or any new statutes in this regard.

9. <u>Taxes & Debts</u>: It is preferred that taxes and debts be paid from other assets of the estate or Trusts of Jane B. Smith rather than the articles owned by this Trust be sold to do so. This is however left to the Successor Trustee's sole discretion.

This Trust Agreement for Personal Property is executed in triplicate and shall be enforced under the laws of Texas. Any copies signed and executed by Jane B. Smith shall be treated the same as an original.

_____

Jane B. Smith

STATE OF TEXAS
COUNTY OF _____

Notary: Jane B. Smith, who appeared before me and was duly sworn, signed this Trust Agreement. She stated she did so of her own free will and appeared to be of sound mind.

        WITNESS my hand and official seal, this _____day of _____A.D. 19_____.

                                _____
                                Signature Notary
                                State of Texas at Large

My commission expires _____

Schedule of Assets

Jane B. Smith's

$1

(See Chapter 8 for a discussion of what to list on Schedule of Assets)

or

1) Diamond Wristwatch

2) Gold, diamond earrings

3) China — Lacepoint by Lennox

4) Sterling silver — Damask Rose by Oneida

5) All other personal possessions, clothing, and household furnishings.

Chapter 14

LIFE INSURANCE

Forty-two (42) of the 500 probate court files studied had life insurance proceeds go through probate. If your estate is the beneficiary of life insurance policies, the proceeds might be subject to your state's inheritance tax. If an individual is the beneficiary, proceeds are usually exempt from state inheritance taxes.

In one of the first estate cases in our study, the primary asset, proceeds of a $25,000 life insurance policy, was left to a sole heir. The estate looked like this:

**9 MONTHS
TIME**

START

$26,616

FINISH
To one heir:
One Check
$24,762

37 PAGES LEGAL WORK

This was caused by the fact the heir was not made the beneficiary of the Life Insurance Policy.

Almost $2,000 disappeared, $1,672 to the attorney alone. The file was 37 pages and involved 9 months time. Making the heir sole beneficiary to the life insurance policy would have been the solution. This gentleman had a Will made approximately two years previous to his death by the same attorney who later "probated" the proceeds. He died in a nursing home at 74 years of age. It was probably apparent to the attorney that he was in poor health.

Had the attorney questioned this man about his assets **and** life insurance policy when the Will was made, he could have suggested the beneficiary of the life insurance policy be changed to his son as sole heir. For giving this advice his fee would have been "**zero**" instead of the $1,672.

It is not wise to make a minor the beneficiary of a life insurance policy because a guardian will probably have to be appointed by the court on the child's behalf. Make someone else the beneficiary or make a trust the beneficiary. Many life insurance companies have trusts already drawn that can be used.

More than one beneficiary can be designated to a life insurance policy. For example, five children could share equally or each receive a percentage. In rare cases, you might want to make your Simple Beneficiary Trust the beneficiary. For example, to enable a business to continue operating after the owner's death and to have cash for operating expenses.

Life insurance policies should be reviewed because beneficiaries may have died, their names changed, etc. Also consider transferring to a new policy with today's interest rates. Older life insurance policies are as obsolete as the 5 1/4% passbook savings account.

Here are suggested wordings to use in regard to beneficiaries on life insurance policies:

ONE BENEFICIARY

Jane B. Smith, wife

TWO BENEFICIARIES

Frank E. Smith, father, and Dorothy M. Smith, mother, equally, or the survivor.

TWO BENEFICIARIES IN UNEQUAL SHARES

Frank E. Smith, father, as to three fourths (3/4) and Dorothy M. Smith, mother, as to one fourth (1/4), or the entire proceeds to the survivor if one is deceased.

THREE OR MORE BENEFICIARIES

Frank E. Smith, father, Dorothy M. Smith, mother, and John C. Smith, Jr., son, or the survivors, equally, or the survivor.

THREE OR MORE BENEFICIARIES
IN UNEQUAL SHARES

Frank E. Smith, father receives one half (1/2), Jane B. Smith, wife, receives one fourth (1/4) and Dorothy M. Smith, mother, receives one-fourth (1/4). The share of any deceased beneficiary is payable to the survivors, proportionate to their original shares. If only one beneficiary survives, then the entire proceeds to that individual.

ONE PRIMARY AND ONE SECONDARY BENEFICIARY

Jane B. Smith, wife, if living; otherwise John C. Smith, Jr., son.

ONE PRIMARY AND TWO SECONDARY BENEFICIARIES

Jane B. Smith, wife, if living; otherwise John C. Smith Jr., son, and Linda Smith Johnson, daughter, equally or the survivor.

ONE PRIMARY AND THREE OR MORE SECONDARY BENEFICIARIES

Jane B. Smith, wife, if living; otherwise John C. Smith, Jr., Linda Smith Johnson and Robert W. Smith, children, or the survivors, equally, or the survivor.

TWO PRIMARY BENEFICIARIES AND ONE SECONDARY BENEFICIARY

Frank E. Smith, father, and Dorothy M. Smith, mother, equally, or the survivor, if either survives; otherwise Jane B. Smith, wife.

ONE PRIMARY BENEFICIARY WITH COMMON DISASTER PROVISION

Jane B. Smith, wife, if she survives the Insured for a

period of ten (10) days; otherwise the children born of the marriage of the Insured and said wife, or the survivors, equally, or the survivor.

TRUSTEE

John C. Smith, Trustee, Under John C. Smith Trust (fill in date trust executed).

PROVISION FOR NAMED CHILDREN AND THEIR ISSUE

Jane B. Smith, wife, if living; otherwise, equally to John C. Smith, Jr., Robert W. Smith, and Linda Smith Johnson, their children. If one child is deceased, his/her children to share equally in that proportionate share.

Chapter 15

REAL ESTATE AND MORTGAGES

There are only two basic ways[19] to have real estate avoid probate:

1. **Joint Tenancy With Right of Survivorship**, or **Tenancy by the Entirety** (Only for husband and wife)

2. **Under your own trust agreement** such as a **Simple Beneficiary Trust**

It is often necessary to have the actual signatures of the owners to transfer property. This could be a disadvantage when using joint ownership. It **cannot** always be solved by each party signing and having notarized a durable power-of-attorney.

The buyer has no way of knowing if you have revoked the power-of-attorney, or if you have been declared legally incompetent since signing it. Wouldn't you be hesitant to take a power-of-attorney for the transfer of the property?

---

[19]There are two others — the unrecorded deed and retaining life estate, but these two should be rarely used. They will however be covered at the end of this chapter.

Powers-of-attorney are used more frequently with commercial property, but rarely in the case of a homestead. Draw up a special power-of-attorney specifying any revocation would have to immediately be recorded to protect the buyer. If you see a possible problem arising, see your attorney.

A deed to property **cannot** be in Jane B. Smith "**OR**" John C. Smith's name. A deed so registered is invalid, it must read "**AND**." Remember from the discussion on bank accounts, the only thing that makes a bank account "**OR**" is a power-of-attorney built into the signature cards. This is not practical for a deed. You may want to change the person to whom you have granted the power-of-attorney, but not wish to change the ownership of the property. If the power-of-attorney were included in the deed, the entire deed would have to be re-registered to revoke it. Because of this, a power-of-attorney must be drawn as a separate document to be used in conjuction with a deed.

The problem of obtaining two signatures does not exist for property held under a Simple Beneficiary Trust. However, joint ownership of property has as its main advantage its simplicity to implement.

The prospect of obtaining a second signature does not usually present a problem. Real estate is not sold at a moment's notice — there is usually ample time to obtain the necessary signatures.

When the beneficiaries are relatives and no cash is involved, the fee to re-register a deed under a trust is minimal. A call to the Recorder of Deeds will verify any details in this regard.

Each deed to property you own must be re-registered so they are governed by your trust. The description of your trust, such as "John C.Smith, Trustee, Under

John C. Smith Trust Dated 3-22-83," must appear on the deed.

It is advisable to record a trust when property is re-registered under that trust. A certified copy of it is necessary when property is sold or when transferred to beneficiaries after your death. The Recorder of Deeds can certify copies from an original that are legally acceptable. I contacted several recorders of documents while writing this book to ask what the charge per page was ($1.00 - $5.00). Since this could get expensive, it would be advisable to consider having your attorney execute 3 copies plus one for each piece of property, and have them. signed while executing your trust agreement.[20]

It is a psychological advantage for husband and wife to register deeds in joint ownership or as co-trustees under a Simple Beneficiary Trust. If a dispute should arise, neither spouse has sole control of the property. Tenancy by the Entirety is for husband and wife and cannot be attached by creditors of each individual, although it can be for debts that are cosigned. A homestead generally cannot be attached by creditors. Consult your attorney/paralegal on the best way to register the deed to avoid probate. You know enough by now to insist on the help and advice you need. For example, if you are married and wish to use joint ownership, does your state recognize Tenancy by the Entirety? If not then you can use JTWROS, or perhaps a trust. For the single and widowed, the Simple Beneficiary Trust is usually preferred.

Make sure the deed is registered in joint ownership, or under a trust agreement to avoid probate. Double check the deed yourself. Review the registrations below that will avoid probate and retain ownership:

[20]The 3 are one for the safe deposit box, one for the recorder of documents, and one extra copy.

John C. Smith and Jane B.
Smith, **Joint Tenancy
with Right of Survivorship**

John C. Smith and Jane B.
Smith, **Tenancy
by the Entirety**
(For husband and wife only)

John C. Smith and Jane B. Smith
**Co-Trustees
Under the John and Mary Smith
Trust Dated 5-26-83**

Mortgages, which are visible evidence of the legal obligation to pay a debt, can easily avoid probate. The two ways to avoid probate are the use of joint ownership, or registration under a trust agreement such as a Simple Beneficiary Trust.

In the case of a **mortgage or a promissory note** which bears a fixed interest rate, and whose immediate **resale value can fluctuate**, it is imperative to avoid probate. This will help prevent a possible forced sale.

If a mortgage for $10,000 at 12% is outstanding for fifteen years, who would pay $10,000 for that mortgage if he could lend the same money out at 16%? The immediate resale value will take into consideration the difference between the interest rate on the mortgage and the prevailing interest rate.

*NOTE: In some states, the deed is automatically in Tenancy by the Entirety even if only "John C. Smith and Jane B. Smith, Husband and Wife" appear on the deed. If Tenancy by the Entirety or Joint Tenancy with Right of Survivorship **does not** appear on the deed, consult your attorney to be sure that the property will avoid probate.*

In one file, I saw a $22,000 mortgage that sold for only $12,000. Interest rates on similar mortgages at the time were paying 16%, but it was set up to pay 10 3/4% and was outstanding for 20 years. Remember, the $10,000 difference was a loss of 45% of the face value; the mortgage was discounted because of the lower interest rate. Interest rates can rapidly vary — Rates decreased from 17% to 12% in a period of five months (August 1982 - December 1982).

If a mortgage is tied up in probate, some states require the proceedings be completed in twelve months or the attorney must file for an extension. To make that petition, he will charge between $60-$150 per hour. The sale of the mortgage could be forced at an inopportune time. All of these problems can be prevented by holding a promissory note or mortgage in joint ownership or under the registrations of a trust. Do not take the risk, forcing your heirs to sell any mortgage or promissory notes at a depressed price, plus lose 6%-22% to probate.

Let us now discuss retaining a life estate in property. This is the right to live in and have use of the property for your lifetime, but have it owned by someone else. The deed must be re-registered to this effect. Ownership of that property has been given up, including the right to sell or borrow money against it. This would normally be used to reduce assets in an estate for tax purposes, or to deprive a spouse of this asset.

Another method sometimes used is the unrecorded deed. Using this technique, the deeds to real estate are made to someone else or to a trust, but are not recorded until after the death of the maker. The unrecorded deed can be reclaimed or destroyed if the maker changes his mind. Some states have title standards against the validity of such transfers and this can be dangerous. One should seek professional advice before considering this method. As we have already discussed, there are safe methods of avoiding probate.

Chapter 16

SAFE DEPOSIT BOXES

The contents of any safe deposit box should be regarded as an asset. Ownership is held in one of five ways:

1. In your name only.
2. Joint Tenancy as "**OR**."
3. Held "**IN TRUST FOR**" utilizing the bank's signature card.[21].
4. By providing the bank a **Simple Beneficiary Trust**, or some **other trust agreement**.
5. By designating a beneficiary (Payment-on-Death/P.O.D) in the 14 states which have the Uniform Probate Code (see Chapter 9 for a list of the states.)

You can be the owner, with a deputy who has power-of-attorney and is allowed access to the box while you are living. The power-of-attorney is included on the account agreement you signed and is made null and void by your death. If there is **only** one owner, the contents of the box will have to go through probate because a deputy is not a co-owner or trustee. Clarify this with the bank.

---

[21]Frequently the signature card will not enumerate anything in regard to the trust as banks acknowledge the words "**IN TRUST FOR**" are indicative enough.

In 100 probate court cases filed in January of 1981 in New York City, 8 needed a court order to open a safe deposit box (1 in 12). If this petition for a court order is obtained through an attorney, it will cost at least one hour of his time plus court costs. In many states, the executor may do this by going to the probate court or writing them for the paperwork and avoid the attorney's fee.

In many states, a safe deposit box registered under a trust is not sealed at death, but is if only in one name, **or** in joint tenancy and one tenant dies. In New Jersey, the box is always sealed. In approximately 1/3 of the states, safe deposit boxes are sealed at death by the inheritance tax department until inventory can be taken with someone from their department present. Each bank's rules and every state's laws can be different. Check with the custodian of the safe deposit department who is often the best counselor on these matters. The rule on ownership of the contents of a safe deposit box is the same for all other assets — **it should never be only in one name** (unless held "**IN TRUST FOR**" or a beneficiary is designated).

To secure burial instructions, deeds to cemetery property, and the Will, a court order can be obtained within a day or two to permit access to the safe deposit box. However, if death occurs on Saturday and a court order is necessary because the box is registered in only one name, this could delay access to the box (4 - 5 days). Even if the box is in "OR", or held in trust, it still could not be opened until Monday. This may be too late for burial instructions. Either keep any funeral instructions accessible at your home or preplan your funeral arrangements.[22]

[22]Counseling on preplanning and prepayment for funerals is available at no charge by contacting your local Funeral or Memorial Society. See your phone directory. If none is listed, write Continental Association of Funeral and Memorial Societies, 2001 "S" St., N.W., Suite 530, Washington, D.C. 20009 and ask for the name and address of the society nearest you. These societies are nonprofit, consumer oriented organizations and are not associated with the funeral industry.

Some valuables should be kept in the safe deposit box. Clarify ownership by registering the box's ownership in "**OR**" (as joint tenants), "**IN TRUST FOR**," or under **your own trust agreement**. If held in "**OR**," it could be assumed both parties owned the contents for inheritance tax purposes. This does not create any problem if the contents are only of personal value, or if no state inheritance tax is due. Owning them under a Simple Beneficiary Trust would solve the problem when the contents are of considerable value and the flexibility of the trust is needed to minimize estate and/or inheritance taxes. The inconvenience of not having some jewelry or other valuables until inventory of the box can be taken should be weighed against the risk of their possible permanent loss or damage.

Always give someone else the right to gain access, **plus** set up ownership of the contents properly to avoid probate, even if they are of limited value. My box's ownership is set up in "**OR**" with my husband, but my mother is appointed as deputy and allowed access. This gives someone access to the box if my husband and I are both unavailable.

Having the bank safe deposit box in "**OR**", or registering the box "**IN TRUST FOR**" or under a **Simple Beneficiary Trust**, will result in the contents avoiding probate. This is the only way to pass unregistered or bearer securities without probate.

Holding your box under a Simple Beneficiary Trust does not allow a second party access to the box, unless you have a co-trustee or appoint someone deputy. Otherwise, access would be allowed only if you were incapacitated and your successor trustee could provide a statement from two licensed physicians in writing. Unfortunately, in 1 out of 3 states a safe deposit box is sealed at death. In a few states, the box is not sealed if held in trust.

Chapter 17

SERIES E AND H BONDS

New bonds being sold are now called Series EE or HH Bonds. These will be referred to by their more familiar name — Series E and H Bonds. As of March 1983, these bonds paid a market-related rate or a minimum of 7 1/2% if held five years. When cashed early during the five-year maturity period, the overall interest rate would be far less. Bonds cannot usually be cashed for six months. "The authority to redeem a bond before the six month waiting period will be granted only in extreme hardship cases."[23]

If they are cashed after the first six months, but before the first year ends, only 4% interest is paid (1 - 2 years, 5 1/2%; 2 - 3 years, 6%; 3 - 4 years, 6 1/2%; and 4 - 5 years, 7%). If cashed during but before the end of any six month interval, you would lose the interest for that 6 months. Only if held five years or longer would you receive the market related rate or 7 1/2%, whichever is higher.

Some of us purchase these bonds through a payroll deduction plan and own them in our name only. If you own bonds and wish to keep them, there are three ways they can avoid probate:

[23]Source: U.S. Treasury

1. "**OR**" with only one co-owner.

2. You can designate one beneficiary.*

3. Re-register under a trust agreement.

One disadvantage of designating a beneficiary, applying only to the old Series E and H Bonds, is this individual must give permission for a change in beneficiaries or, if deceased, then his/her death certificate must be provided. The new Series EE and HH bonds do not require the present beneficiary's permission to change beneficiary or if deceased, their death certificate.

Disadvantages to "**OR**" are that the second party can cash the Series E (EE) or H (HH) Bonds on his signature alone. Since he is a joint owner, the bonds cannot be left to anyone else by your Will. Be sure this is your intent. Advantages are that only one signature is needed to cash them in and they avoid probate.

On the back of the bonds it is stated they are not transferable. Also, they cannot be used as collateral. Ownership can be transferred only to certain relatives.[24] As long as you remain part owner, the bond can be re-registered in "**OR**", or under a trust. To change the registration to "**OR**", to a trust, or to designate a beneficiary on Series E (EE) or H (HH) bonds, you must return the bond(s) with the appropriate completed U. S. Government form. Forms are available at most commercial banks or by writing to the following address:

> Department of the Treasury
> Bureau of Public Debt
> 200 3rd Street
> Parkersburg, W.Va. 26101
> 1-304-422-8551

*This is the same as Payment on Death or P.O.D.

[24]**Federal Register**, Vol. 44 No. 248, Dec. 26, 1979, page 76450

Chapter 18

A BUSINESS THAT IS
A SOLE PROPRIETORSHIP

Some businesses are not incorporated because this creates additional paperwork and added expense. The **only** way a sole proprietorship can avoid probate is when owned under a trust, such as the Simple Beneficiary Trust or a separate trust.

A business that is a sole proprietorship can have many assets, like inventory and good will, with no evidence of ownership by a deed or title. For this reason and because it is owned by one individual, it can avoid probate only by use of a trust. When equipment or inventory is purchased, the invoice should list the purchaser as your trust. Invoices could be construed to be a title.

In the text of a Simple Beneficiary Trust, a paragraph after contingent beneficiary could refer to any business as follows:

Special: The beneficiary and sole owner of all assets and the business known as Smith's Gift & Card Shop at Jane B. Smith's death is her daughter, Linda Smith Johnson.

A separate trust agreement for your sole proprietorship might be considered because it could take time to sell the business or liquidate assets. A separate trust will allow it to continue under someone else's management and avoid probate. You understand the nature of your business, so you are in the best position to make this decision. All other assets can be registered under joint tenancy; a sole proprietorship cannot.

The bank account and any accounts at other financial institutions should be re-registered as follows:

Smith's Gift & Card Shop   (24 characters)

Owned by Jane B. Smith TTEE*   (27 characters)

Jane B. Smith U.T.D.** 5-14-83   (28 characters)

Thirty-two characters and spaces are the maximum one line can hold for the personalization of a check. Four lines are available for a personal account, if pressed check companies will allow five lines, the usual for a business. Note: the above illustration uses three lines and clearly denotes the account is for the business.

*Abbreviation for Trustee
**Abbreviation for Under Trust Dated

The following is a reference trust to use when writing a separate trust for business:

TRUST AGREEMENT

of

Jane B. Smith

for

Smith's Gift & Card Shop

I, Jane B. Smith, a resident of St. Louis County, Minnesota and being of sound mind, make this Trust Agreement of my own free will and revoke any Trust Agreements for Sole Proprietorship Businesses I previously executed, and any amendments to these prior Trust Agreements for Sole Proprietorship Businesses.

1. <u>Trust Purpose</u>: Assets owned by this Trust, which includes Smith's Gift and Card Shop, are held in trust for the benefit of Jane B. Smith's daughter, Linda Smith Johnson. If she is deceased, or unwilling to receive the vehicles owned by this Trust, then the beneficiary shall be her children to share equally. Jane B. Smith may use any principal and income from assets owned by this Trust for her comfort, support, general welfare, health and education.

2. <u>Trust Name and Property</u>: This Trust shall be known as the "Jane B. Smith Trust Dated 5-14-83 for Smith's Gift and Card Shop." The above shop, located at 1017 E. Colonial Avenue, Duluth, Minnesota, and owned in its entirety by Jane B. Smith, is held in Trust under this Agreement. Jane B. Smith the Grantor (Owner) is also the Trustee.

3. <u>Successor Trustee</u>: In the event that Jane B. Smith is incapacitated as certified in writing by two licensed physicians or is deceased, then her daughter, Linda Smith Johnson, shall be Successor Trustee. If Linda Smith Johnson is deceased, or is unable or unwilling to serve as Successor Trustee, the Successor Trustee shall be Jane B. Smith's granddaughter, Margaret Johnson. Any Successor Trustee agrees to serve with no compensation, unless it is agreed to by all beneficiaries.

4. <u>Management</u>: The Trustee or any Successor Trustee is authorized to operate, sell, terminate, or enter into contracts for the business at her sole and absolute discretion. Jane B. Smith, the Trustee, or any Successor Trustee, shall have all the powers Jane B. Smith would have if she were acting as a legally competent individual, and still owned the business only in her name. This includes the right to borrow against or pledge these assets — including the right to mortgage real estate or margin stocks.

5. <u>Right to Revoke or Change</u>: Jane B. Smith reserves the right to revoke, amend or make changes to this Trust Agreement at any point during her lifetime.

6. <u>Creditors</u>: The assets owned by this Trust are not accessible in any way by creditors of her beneficiaries, Successor Trustee or their past or present spouses.

7. <u>Bond and Accounting</u>: No bond shall be required of the Trustee or any Successor Trustee. The Trustee or Successor Trustee is not required to make any accounting as required under Minnesota Rule 28 or any changes to that

Rule in the future, or similar Rules or Statute(s) that might be enacted in regard to accounting for Trusts. The Successor Trustee can keep records and do accounting as she deems reasonable.

8. Taxes and Debts: If Jane B. Smith is incapacitated or deceased, the Trust assets may be used by the Successor Trustee to pay her personal and/or business debts and/or taxes due as the Successor Trustee deems proper and reasonable.

9. Disappearance: Jane B. Smith and/or any subsequent beneficiary shall be presumed dead if after two years she has not been heard from, and the body is not recovered. All assets and income owned by this Trust may then be distributed. The Successor Trustee can manage assets as provided in this Trust, during that two year period.

This Trust Agreement for the Sole Proprietorship Business known as Smith's Gift and Card Shop was executed in triplicate in Minnesota and shall be enforced under the laws of that State. Any copies signed and executed by Jane B. Smith shall be treated the same as an original.

_____

Jane B. Smith

_____   _____

Witness   Witness

_____   _____

Street   Street

_____   _____

City   State   City   State

STATE OF MINNESOTA
COUNTY OF _____

Notary: Jane B. Smith, who appeared before me and who was duly sworn, signed this Trust Agreement. She stated she did so of her own free will, and she appeared to be of sound mind.

       WITNESS my hand and official seal, this _____day of _____A.D. 19_____.

                               _____
                               Signature Notary
                               State of Minnesota at Large

My commission expires _____

Schedule of Assets

Smith's Card and Gift Shop

Chapter 19

STOCK AND BOND CERTIFICATES AND BROKERAGE ACCOUNTS

There are three ways to avoid probate with brokerage accounts or securities (stocks and bonds):

1. **Joint Tenancy with Right of Survivorship (JTWROS)** or **Tenancy by the Entirety**.[25] These accounts or certificates are "**AND**."

2. New cash management accounts[26] offered by the brokerage firms make these accounts equivalent to "**OR**" accounts at the banks, but if you read the account agreements, they are also **JTWROS**. Access to money in the account is provided by checks needing one signature or a cash advance on a credit card.

3. A trust agreement provided by you such as a Simple Beneficiary Trust. Brokerage firms, unlike banks, will not register an account "**IN TRUST FOR**" unless you provide them with your own separately written trust agreement.

[25]Tenancy by the Entirety is rarely seen in security registrations for very complex reasons. Brokerage firms prefer accounts and certificates to be registered in **JTWROS** rather than Tenancy by the Entirety. A specific request to do otherwise will have to be submitted to the firm.

[26]These accounts are called; CMA Accounts/Cash Management Accounts at Merrill Lynch, or AAA Accounts at Dean Witter Reynolds.

A possible first step to make things easier for your family: keep all securities "in street name" at the brokerage house. I call it "on deposit" since it is equivalent to depositing money in the bank. The banker does not keep every bill with a little note clipped to it as to who owns it. The brokerage firm has certificates re-registered in the firm's name. You are given a receipt for the certificates, and they then appear on your subsequent statements. It is all a matter of processing by computers. At several major brokerage firms there is a $10 charge every six months for this service but **only** if there is no activity. The charge will rarely occur because most people will have a deposit or withdrawal to their money market fund. Even if charged the fee is minimal, to insure the safekeeping of your securities, bookkeeping, and records done for income tax purposes.

The advantage of placing certificates on deposit with a brokerage firm is explained in the following example. In two estates, both owning 30 securities, one had all on deposit and the account in JTWROS; the other held each security certificate individually in JTWROS. The first required one death certificate to transfer ownership and the second — 30 death certificates, the charges for certified mail, and a lot of time to send 30 different certificates to the respective transfer agents. When stocks are kept on deposit with the brokerage firm, that firm holds the certificates in their name. Discount brokers will also hold securities on deposit and usually provide this service free.

A person may be in the habit of "holding" certificates, however. This was common before brokerage accounts were insured for up to $500,000 (including $100,000 in cash) by a federal agency. Inquire as to whether your brokerage account is covered by the S.I.P.C. (Securities Investors Protection Corporation). Safe deposit boxes at home or in banks can be broken into and the contents may not be insured.

One brokerage firm that was covered by S.I.P.C. insurance failed recently. Because the firm kept poor records, there was a delay of months before some clients obtained their certificates. You can insure against this by dealing with a large, well established firm. However, there is always a remote possibility of this occurring, Goodbody & Co., a major firm did fail many years ago.

Advantages of leaving securities on deposit with a brokerage firm are numerous. A statement will be received a minimum of once every four months, and the firm will automatically enclose educational brochures. New opportunities in money management are always occurring, and may be beneficial. Dividends and interest are paid automatically into the account. Arrangements can be made for dividends and interest paid to be deposited in a money market fund.

Placing certificates on deposit with a brokerage firm can create a psychological disadvantage if you decide to sell these securities through another stockbroker. You may feel obligated to transact business with the firm holding your certificates rather than executing the proper paperwork that allows another broker to sell them.

Talk to your stockbroker, and have him explain the benefits of keeping securities on deposit with his firm. You might decide this is an excellent way to make sure that your family will have to give the brokerage house only one death certificate to effect transfer. This will occur if the account is in **JTWROS**, or registered under a Simple Beneficiary Trust, and **all securities are on deposit with the brokerage firm**.

We have already discussed **JTWROS** and the Simple Beneficiary Trust. Once you have your securities "on deposit" it is only necessary to send a letter of instruction with the signatures of the owner(s) of the account to the firm with a photostat of the trust. There is a sample letter at the end of this chapter.

Cash management accounts at brokerage houses make access to money in accounts the same as the "**OR**" privilege at banks and offer many other helpful services. Checks are provided for either party allowing any amount up to the credit limit in the account to be withdrawn. You may also have a major credit card for cash advances.

To open these accounts requires a minimum of $20,000 in securities (stocks and bonds) and/or cash. As little as $2,500 in cash and/or securities, (less at account executive's discretion), is required to keep them open.

A discount broker, Charles Schwab & Co., is offering a similar account needing only a minimum of $5,000 in cash and/or securities to open. Fidelity, a company which owns a family of mutual funds and offers discount broker-age services, has one that requires $10,000 to open. As standard procedure, they also return cancelled checks. "Shop" around for the best cash management account by watching the financial section of the local paper, the Wall Street Journal, and such publications as Business Week, Financial World, Forbes, Fortune, and Money Magazine.

Mutual funds, or money market funds **other** than those connected with brokerage house's cash management ac-counts, are the only instances I know in which a power-of-attorney is not accepted. However, these can be re-regis-tered under a Simple Beneficiary Trust. Trust agreements are not provided automatically.

Since the money market fund has to be "**AND**," and a power-of-attorney will not be accepted, the problem can be solved by signing a few checks for each other for the time when the second party is unavailable. In the case of a mutual fund, have a stock power signed, then the mutual fund shares can be liquidated.

When stock certificates are kept in your possession, the signatures are more likely to pose a problem. Any inconvenience can be prevented by having stock powers signed. Your stockbroker will provide these forms free of charge and instructions about signature guarantees. They can also be purchased at any stationery store. Only the signature is required; leave it to the brokerage firm to fill out the rest. These forms are the same as signing the certificate. The stock/bond powers are useful only when attached to the actual certificate and sent to the mutual fund or money market fund with a letter of instruction which you would send at the time you wish to cash them in.

ASSIGNMENT SEPARATE FROM SECURITY

For Value Received, the undersigned hereby sell(s), assign(s), and transfer(s) to

_____

IF STOCK, COMPLETE THIS PORTION

_____ shares of the _____ stock of _____

represented by Certificate No(s) _____

standing in the name of the undersigned on the books of said Corporation.

IF BOND, COMPLETE THIS PORTION

one bond of the_____

in the principal amount of $ _____, No(s) _____

standing in the name of the undersigned on the books of said Corporation.

The undersigned does (do) hereby irrevocably constitute and appoint_____

_____ Attorney to transfer the said stock(s), bond, or debenture(s),

as the case may be on the books of said Corporation with full power of substitution in the premises.

OFFICE	ACCOUNT NO.	A.E.
RECEIPT NO.		

Signed _____

Dated _____   Signed _____

If you are concerned about whether any mutual funds or securities you own will avoid probate, check with your stockbroker. If you do not have a broker, call any firm and explain your concern (preferably a member of the New York Stock Exchange which requires a lengthy training program before licensing a broker). Make an appointment to discuss alternatives. There is no charge for this service.

A primary and contingent beneficiary may be designated on Individual Retirement and Keogh Accounts held at a brokerage firm. However, you cannot designate a beneficiary on other brokerage accounts at present.

Dean Witter Reynolds
1 Boston Plaza
Boston, Mass. 02108

RE: Jane B. Smith
     Acc't: 440-62036-0-26

Dear Sir:

Please re-register my above account to read as follows:

Jane B. Smith TTEE
Jane B. Smith U.T.D. 11-17-83

Please advise me if a new account number as been assigned. I can be reached during business hours at 649-2223.

Thank you.

           Sincerely,

           Jane B. Smith

*For a way to pass bearer or unregistered securities without probate, see Chapter 16.

Chapter 20

VEHICLES WITH A TITLE
AS EVIDENCE OF OWNERSHIP

In most states, cars and other vehicles are exempt from probate. However, the auto tag agency will require notarized affidavits proving right to ownership, statements of release from other heirs, and a copy of the death certificate. When other assets are registered to avoid probate, it is not necessary to re-register vehicles under a trust because they are usually of limited value. You will own many cars before your death, and it creates extra paperwork to always have the titles registered under a trust. The reason joint tenancy is not recommended for a car will be discussed later in this chapter.

Reference has been made to Disposition Without Administration (Chapter 4), which is generally for estates of $5,000 or less and does not require the services of an attorney. In the following example, where the car caused the estate to exceed the $5,000 limit, the problem was created by other assets NOT being set up to avoid probate — NOT by the car.

Bank Account	$2,452
Stock	2,100
VALUE OF CAR	**1,400**
	$5,952

TITLES TO VEHICLES SHOULD NOT BE IN JOINT TENANCY WHICH IS PRACTICAL IN MOST SITUATIONS, BUT NOT HERE. THIS IS BECAUSE OF POTENTIAL LIABILITY. If a vehicle is in joint names and an accident occurs, both owners can be held liable. If the vehicle is in one name only, or registered under a Simple Beneficiary Trust with a single trustee, there is only one owner liable.

If you have a Simple Beneficiary Trust, providing there is only one trustee, then you can choose to register all vehicles under it (including campers, motorcycles, recreational vehicles, boats, etc). If there are several, it can all be done in one trip to the auto tag agency. HOWEVER, CONSULT AN ATTORNEY BEFORE REGISTERING VEHICLES UNDER A TRUST IF THERE ARE CO-TRUSTEES; YOU BOTH COULD BE HELD LIABLE.

Exception: A stationary vehicle (mobile home) is generally treated as a vehicle and can be registered 1) "OR," 2) "AND," or 3) under a Simple Beneficiary Trust. Check with your local auto tag agency to determine the status of a mobile home in your state. If the mobile home is treated in your state as a homestead, see Chapter 15 on real estate. For the advantages and disadvantages of "OR", "AND", or joint ownership see Chapter 7.

The following is a sample trust for vehicles, to be used only when all other assets are held in joint ownership:

TRUST AGREEMENT

for

Vehicles

of

Jane B. Smith

I, Jane B. Smith, a resident of Santa Clara County, California and being of sound mind, make this Trust Agreement for Vehicles and revoke any Trust Agreement for Vehicles I previously executed, and any amendments to those prior Trust Agreements for Vehicles.

1. Trust Purpose: Jane B. Smith shall have the use and all benefits from any vehicles owned by the Trust for her lifetime. She may sell any vehicles owned by this Trust and use the proceeds as she sees fit. Another purpose is to designate beneficiaries to the vehicles owned by the Trust at

Jane B. Smith's death and provide for a Successor Trustee in the event she is deceased or is incapacitated as defined. At Jane B. Smith's death, the Successor Trustee is to distribute all assets owned by this Trust and this Trust terminates.

2. Trust Name and Property: This Trust shall be known as the "Jane B. Smith Trust Dated 6-22-83 for Vehicles." All titles to Vehicles which are registered "Jane B. Smith, Trustee Under Jane B. Smith Trust Dated 6-22-83 for Vehicles" or an abbreviated version of this shall be governed by the terms and conditions as specified herein.

3. Beneficiaries: At the death of Jane B. Smith, the primary beneficiary of vehicles registered under this Trust shall be John C. Smith, her husband. The contingent beneficiary at her death shall be her father, James E. Brown.

4. Successor Trustee: In the event that Jane B. Smith is incapacitated as certified in writing by two licensed physicians or is deceased the Successor Trustee shall be John C. Smith. In the event John C. Smith is deceased, or unable or unwilling to serve, then the Successor Trustee shall be James E. Brown. The Successor Trustee agrees to serve without compensation unless it is agreed to by all the beneficiaries.

5. Management: Jane B. Smith, the Trustee, or any Successor Trustee, shall have all powers that Jane B. Smith would have if she were mentally competent and still owned all vehicles of the Trust only in her name. This includes the right to borrow against or pledge as collateral these vehicles, including the right to change insurance.

6. Right to Revoke, Bond, Accounting and Creditors: Jane B. Smith retains the right to change all or part of this Trust during her lifetime. No bond or accounting shall be required of her or any Successor Trustee. The assets owned

by this Trust are not accessible in any way by creditors of her beneficiaries, Successor Trustee, or their past or present spouses.

This Trust Agreement for Vehicles was executed in triplicate in California and shall be enforced under the laws of that state. Any copies signed and executed by Jane B. Smith shall be treated the same as an original.

_____

Jane B. Smith

STATE OF CALIFORNIA
COUNTY OF _____

NOTARY: Jane B. Smith, who appeared before me and was duly sworn, signed this Trust Agreement. She stated that she did so of her own free will and appeared to be of sound mind.

      WITNESS my hand and official seal, this _____day of _____A.D. 19_____.

                              _____
                              Signature Notary
                              State of California at Large

My commission expires _____

Schedule of Assets

1982 Mercury Cougar

Since cars or other vehicles are usually of limited value, a Notary should be sufficient. However, when they are of considerable value, go through the same procedures and statements as on the Simple Beneficiary Trust.

When a new car is purchased, present the trust agreement to the salesman or the dealership **before** the title is issued and advise him how to word the registration. For example: "Jane B. Smith, TTEE*, Jane B. Smith U.T.D.** 6-22-83 for Vehicles."

*Abbreviation for Trustee
**Abbreviation for Under Trust Dated

Chapter 21

POWERS-OF-ATTORNEY

People who own assets in joint tenancy should always provide each other with a power-of-attorney. At every bank where you hold an account in "**OR**," you signed a power-of-attorney built into the signature card. Every financial institution has preprinted powers-of-attorney. All you have to do is ask.

A durable power-of-attorney, valid even if you are incapacitated, sounds attractive on the surface but it can be difficult to compose. Carefully read the sample in this chapter. If you are willing to go to this much trouble, I suggest that you have a Simple Beneficiary Trust drawn. You should have an attorney/paralegal draw either document. A power-of-attorney may prevent a guardianship, but does nothing to help assets avoid probate. There are approximately 50 times more probate cases than guardianship cases. **Remember, any power-of-attorney is made null and void by your death.**

Institutions may require a power-of-attorney to refer to the type asset under their jurisdiction. Below is a reprint from the <u>Federal Register</u> illustrating this:

Powers of Attorney

The new savings bond regulations permit limited recognition of powers of attorney to cash bonds where the grantor has specifically authorized the attorney-in-fact to sell or redeem Treasury securities and the power of attorney containing such authority has been executed before a certifying officer. The more common power of attorney will be recognized only in those cases where the grantor has become mentally incompetent or physically disabled, provided the power specifically provides for this contingency. These two provisions operate independently of one another.

Specifically referring to every possibility makes a durable power-of-attorney far more complex to compose than a trust. The very same issue of the <u>Federal Register</u> makes no such requirements of trust agreements nor did instructional booklets from any financial institutions.

A durable power-of-attorney is made null and void in some states if you are declared legally incompetent. Even in states where the Uniform Probate Code is in effect, it still requires the agent appointed by the durable power-of-attorney to report to your guardian, who in turn reports to the court. **If your care is being paid for, no one will normally force your family to have you declared legally incompetent.** A durable power-of-attorney would give someone access to your assets to pay for care as needed.

A special durable power-of-attorney could allow your assets to be placed in a trust if you were incapacitated. However, it is preferable to establish a trust while you are well and capable of making the arrangements yourself. This sample durable power-of-attorney incorporates the provisions of a durable health power-of-attorney for you but so does the Simple Beneficiary Trusts.

DURABLE POWER-OF-ATTORNEY

I, Jane B. Smith, residing at 1025 Abby Lane, New York, New York, do appoint my husband, John C. Smith, or son, John C. Smith, Jr., who may act individually under this power-of-attorney as my Agent to perform for me at any point during my lifetime the following:

A. To withdraw and deposit money(ies) in accounts I have at any bank, savings and loan association, credit union, or other institution. Also, to collect money due from insurance companies, governmental agencies, trustees, or other debtors and give receipts.

B. To disburse money(ies) withdrawn or paid on my behalf:

1. To pay for care by hospitals, nursing homes, physicians, and all others deemed necessary.

2. For medical, hospital, life, auto, homeowner's, property, and liability insurance presently owned or deemed necessary.

3. Expenditures for the maintenance and protection of my assets.

4. For debts and taxes.

5. Compensation to my Agent for of out-of-pocket expenses. Reasonable expenses will be allowed, such expenditures must be approved by both. Since both are close family members, this is inserted in case of extraordinary circumstances.

6. Customary donations to church and charities if assets permit.

C. To make tax returns and apply for exemptions and refunds.

D. To select and employ physicians, nurses, nursing homes, hospitals and others as necessary or terminate their employment.

E. To make claims for medical, governmental, employee insurance and other benefits. To elect options for these benefits; bring suits to enforce my rights, or defend and compromise suits against me.

F. To endorse and deposit at any bank, savings and loan association, stock brokerage firm, credit union, other institution, or escrow account, checks payable to me and any cash.

G. To invest funds in money market accounts or certificate of deposit at any bank, savings and loan association, brokerage firm or credit union. Also to buy and sell U.S. Treasury bills. (U.S. Treasury notes and bonds were not included. The reasons are: long term obligations, resale value fluctuates as interest rates vary, and they require large minium purchases or fees are usually prohibitive).

H. To enter my safe deposit boxes, remove contents, place documents, jewelry or other assets therein, and renew or terminate leases of safe deposit boxes.

I. To sell or buy rights to purchase stocks and bonds, exercise rights for me, and vote by proxy or in person shares of stock owned by me.

J. To transfer, buy or sell any U.S. Series E (EE) or H (HH) Bonds.

K. To terminate instructions issued to mutual funds, stock brokerage firms, agents, trustees and others regarding: 1)investing income, dividends, and capital gains 2)disbursements to me, and issuing new instructions necessary to satisfy my financial needs.

L. To enter real estate contracts to sell, buy, rent and manage. Also to repair, improve, alter and insure any buildings thereon. To contract for leasing for any periods, rents and conditions my Agent deems proper and reasonable and any proceedings against tenants.

M. To sign written instructions and consents required or recommended by physician(s), hospital, nursing home, or other facility. Also in making prearrangements with a mortician.

N. To arrange for care and disposition of pets.

O. To change my mailing address.

P. To issue orders stopping payment of checks drawn on my account.

Q. To exercise protective custody over assets.

R. To deliver, in the case I am moved to new quarters, items of my personal property into the custody of those chosen.

S. To sell, buy, assign, transfer, convey, deliver, mortgage, lease, exchange, and trade any or all of my shares of common and preferred stocks, bonds, debentures, real property (real estate), and other assets of every form and nature; to borrow money and repay same; and perform other acts within the scope of this broadest general power-of-attorney, unlimited by recital of specific powers. This includes the right to mortgage or pledge real estate and margin stocks.

I grant my Agent full power and authority to do everything I would do. I relieve my Agent of liability for losses arising out of errors in judgment while acting for me hereunder in good faith.

This power-of-attorney shall continue in full force and effect until either a) I shall have passed away or b) ten (10) days shall have elapsed after the recording of revocation which must be done at the Public Recorder of New York County, State of New York.

Each executed copy shall be construed as an original.

I subscribe my name this _____day of _____, 19_____.

_____
Jane B. Smith

STATE OF NEW YORK
COUNTY OF NEW YORK

NOTARY: Jane B. Smith, who appeared before me and was duly sworn, signed this Durable Power-of-Attorney. She stated she did so of her own free will and she appeared to be of sound mind.

WITNESS my hand and official seal, this _____day of _____A.D. 19_____

_____
Signature Notary
State of New York at Large

My commission expires _____

Witness: _____

Address: _____   Accepted _____
                                            Agent

_____
City   State

Witness: _____

Address: _____   Accepted _____
                                            Agent

_____
City   State

Chapter 22

STATE INHERITANCE TAXES

There are no state inheritance taxes, in essence, if you live in one of the following states or American Samoa:

Alabama	Missouri
Alaska	Montana**
Arizona	Nevada
Arkansas	New Mexico
California	North Dakota
Colorado	Oregon***
Florida	Texas
Georgia	Utah
Hawaii	Vermont
Illinois	Virginia
Maine*	Washington
Minnesota	Wyoming

(Always make sure your state has not changed its inheritance tax status.)

*Maine's inheritance tax will be phased out by July 1, 1986 leaving only the Federal Credit.

**Nonlineal descendants (aunts, uncles, nieces, nephews, and cousins) are not eligible for as high an exemption.

***Oregon's estate tax will be phased out by Jan. 1, 1987 leaving only the Federal Credit.

All of these states (except Nevada) are structured so the state receives funds only from the federal estate tax revenue sharing program. The state receives a portion of what has to be paid to the federal government. In reality, these states have no inheritance tax. Remaining states have inheritance taxes, and local advice should be obtained.

When it appears this type tax is owed, contact the nearest inheritance tax office and ask them to send any brochures or pamphlets describing these taxes. Call the inheritance tax office and ask questions on anything you do not fully understand. These questions might be helpful:

1. Are safe deposit boxes sealed at death if held jointly? If held under a trust?

2. Are bank accounts frozen at death if held jointly? If held under a trust?

3. Are there any savings on inheritance taxes if assets are held jointly? (In many states there are, at times making joint ownership the best decision. For example, in Michigan, bank accounts held jointly by any parties are exempt from the state inheritance tax if held this way at least two years prior to death. They are not exempt if left by a trust or Will.)

4. If considering joint tenancy, will this result in double taxation? (For example, will the asset be taxed 100% at the first tenant's death and then 100% when the second tenant dies? This rarely occurs for spouses, but could for others such as parent and child.)

Joint ownership is so commonly used that often a written statement (affidavit) that the property was owned 100% by the surviving tenant is sufficient to avoid inheritance taxes. No additional proof is necessary if your explanation sounds reasonable to the inheritance tax department. In other states, you must be able to provide "proof of contribution."

My associates visited the inheritance tax offices in several states and found little conflict in setting up assets to avoid probate. The average paid in state inheritance taxes of the 500 probate court cases studied was $1,105 versus $7,800 in probate expenses!

No state inheritance taxes were due on 278 of the 500 cases included in our study. There is a trend developing to relieve most of us from these taxes. After all — the small amounts collected from middle class citizens is not worth the paperwork.

Your record keeping will go smoothly with the help of the record book offered at the back of this book. Leave your heirs a record of where your bank accounts are, approximate amounts, and account numbers. The same records will facilitate filling out inheritance tax returns.

Chapter 23

ADVICE TO PEOPLE
WITH MINOR CHILDREN

People with minor children must be careful of holding assets in one name only. If you die without a Will, a spouse usually receives 1/2 the assets, and the children 1/2. If the children are minors, the surviving spouse often must be appointed legal guardian of his/her own children and give an accounting to the court annually. Not to mention that a guardianship will involve the expense of an annual bond, court costs, and an attorney's fee to process necessary paperwork. This may not be necessary if there are only a few thousand dollars involved, but the investment of those funds will be severely restricted.

There are many persons who "mean well", but do not realize a guardianship will be necessary in the event of death. For instance, if your brother makes you and your minor child beneficiaries to a life insurance policy and other company benefits, it is a mistake. It is best for you to request to be sole beneficiary (or that assets be left to a trust) to avoid a guardianship.

A Will is a necessity to be sure any miscellaneous assets go to a spouse, or a trust on behalf of the children. If a parent dies without designating someone or a trust (already set up, or set up by the Will) to receive miscellaneous assets, a guardianship might be required for them even if all other assets have been registered to avoid probate. Suppose you are killed in an accident with someone else at fault, the award for damages (a check issued after your death) must go through probate. Only a Will can designate a person or a trust to receive this check. Another important purpose of a Will is to state a preference for a legal guardian if both parents predecease their minor children. Any appointment is the final decision of the court, but your stated preference is given first consideration.

If there is only one parent and limited assets, you might register them jointly with whomever you appointed legal guardian of your children in your Will. This will also prevent probate and guardianship of assets. If there are substantial assets involved, then a Simple Beneficiary Trust is advisable. The trust is a legal entity owning the assets and the children are beneficiaries. Because of the trust, a third party (trustee) has been given management responsibility until the children are 18 or reach an appointed age. Unless you specify it, the trustee reports to no one. Then if the trustee does not manage funds properly the framework is ready for legal recourse.

Beware — with minor children, assets should not be registered only in one name or left to be inherited by them. If assets are set up to avoid probate, they are managed by the surviving spouse or a trust rather than dictated by a guardianship. Also, a guardianship releases assets to a child at age 18 who may not have the insight to wisely invest them. Frequently, Wills drawn by attorneys leave assets to minor children. This creates guardianships and an annual annuity for the legal profession.

ADDENDUM

All 50 states and the District of Columbia have passed the Uniform Gifts to Minors Act. This Act allows asset(s) to be held by a custodian on a minor's behalf without court supervision or a trust. Its primary advantage is that minors have a lower tax rate. Any income is taxable to the minors as they are legally the owners of the asset(s) and have the right to full possession of same at age 18. If the child dies, the asset(s) will have to go through probate. A remote possibility usually not worth worrying about if the child is in good health. Even if this occurs, the paperwork can be done with the help of a clerk at the probate court if under your state's limit (average $5,000.)

If the custodian dies, the minor (if 14) can usually designate a new custodian. If the custodian is elderly or in poor health and the child is under 14, check your state's statutes on leaving a letter designating a new custodian.

Chapter 24

HOW TO EMPLOY AN ATTORNEY

This is a day and age of specialization, so **confirm** if the attorney you have contacted has experience in making trusts **before** you set the appointment. For instance, you would not want an attorney specializing in corporate law who has never done a trust. Of the 617,000 attorneys in this country — 9 out of 10 have rarely made a trust!

In general, how does one find an attorney? Nothing beats recommendations based on personal experience. If none of your friends know an attorney knowledgeable in the area in which you need help, look in the Yellow Pages under attorneys by specialty. **There is an overabundance of them**. You will probably find a multitude offering a free first visit, a symptom of a very overcrowded field. Avoid those who spend fortunes on advertising. Blatant ads are probably run by only 5% of attorneys in practice. A truly good attorney can best be found by word of mouth which keeps them busy enough. My attorney explained that he made a list of ten attorneys he would retain if he needed legal help — not one had anything more than a discrete ad. A point well taken.

You may call the Lawyer Referral Service. However, this is an absolute last resort. You will get the next attorney "up" on their list — not necessarily someone with experience and expertise in your particular problem. Some cities have privately run referral services that do a better job of locating someone for you in the field or with the experience you need. They are listed in the Yellow Pages under attorneys.

When you think you have found the right attorney, inform him you will only consider employing him on an hourly basis and ask about his charge (normally $60-$150 per hour). It might seem high but remember the attorney has overhead to pay. Be organized; know the type of help you need. Complete the asset and checklist at the end of this book in preparation for your consultation. If you need a Simple Beneficiary Trust, take a photostat of the one from this book and fill in your own names and information. The less he has to do, the less his fees should be. You might pay a flat fee for 1) a trust 2) Will 3) re-registering assets. A fee of $300 to $500 would be considered fair (1983 prices) for performing all 3 services.

A gimmick attorneys often use is to charge a flat fee of $750 to $1,500 for counseling on estate planning and to make a trust and/or Will. One tried to charge me that even though the charge had verbally been agreed upon at $75 an hour. I wrote him that I could see only a maximum of two hours of his time spent and that I knew the trust and Will he had prepared for me was done on a word processor. He then agreed to accept what I thought was fair. I will never make a verbal agreement with an attorney after this episode. The trust and Will were also much too lengthy — eighteen pages long! Of course, they took a secretary only about 20 minutes with the help of a word processor.

With the exception of very complicated cases, do not employ an attorney on a percentage basis; agree on an hourly rate.[27] I met a lady soon after starting this book who had agreed to pay an attorney 5% of her husband's assets

---

[27]In states with statutes permitting a percentage basis, in most cases shop until you find one that agrees to an hourly fee.

to probate his estated **including** life insurance policies on which she was the beneficiary. That 5% was almost $10,-000 for an estimated twenty hours of time to probate the estate (five hundred dollars an hour)! Because she had no idea the amount of time or work it would take or what was a fair fee, she **trusted** the attorney to charge her fairly. A charge of $60-$150 an hour is **enough**. Tell the attorney you will expect an accounting of his time. Keep a notebook recording the date and time of **every visit** and **phone conversation**. Confirm that you both agree on the time expended at the end of a phone conversation or conference. Request a monthly billing or a billing when the charges exceed $100. It is popular to charge for fifteen minutes even if phone conversations only last thirty seconds. Taking into account the time necessary to record your call, a minimum charge of 6 minutes could be allowed.

Your attorney could try to charge for research such as reading the statutes. The general rule is that he is expected to be knowledgeable in something as common as the probate statutes and should not learn them at your expense. Why does an attorney think his time is worth $60-$150 an hour unless he is being paid for his knowledge? One hour for review of the statutes would be permissible. Tell him ahead of time — a refresher maybe, an education no.

Be sure to sign a contract before work is begun, stating: 1) fee on time spent basis, 2) periodic accounting of his time, and 3) an estimate of time needed. **Get it in writing up front to avoid any misunderstanding.** For more complicated legal problems, it is best to pay monthly for work performed. If a retainer is required, a refund may not be given in a disagreement over charges. Also, a better record of his time can be kept with a monthly or quarterly accounting or billing.

Examine the file of the estate you have retained an attorney to probate. If the file is inaccessible, write the court where it is on file, requesting the number of pages in the file and the charge per page. Then send them a check. It is not enough to instruct the attorney to send you a photostat of everything filed. You should check with the probate court every three months and pay them to send you copies of any additional paperwork filed. **You will understand much better what is going on if you do this and take less of the attorney's time**. The charge per page for photostating at probate courts may range from 25 cents to $1. Even if the file is 50-100 pages, it will usually be worth the investment. Since attorneys charge $60-$150 an hour, if having the actual files saves you only one hour of his time, you will have recovered the cost of getting the file photostated. The attorney will have to explain far less to you if you have a photostat of the paperwork. Also, call the probate court with any questions before taking the attorney's time.

Chapter 25

WHOM TO CHOOSE AS YOUR SUCCESSOR TRUSTEE AND/OR EXECUTOR

Responsibilities of a successor trustee and/or executor have become less complicated since there is no need to file the 16 page federal estate tax return in the majority of cases. Now up to $600,000 will be exempt from federal estate taxes in 1987 compared to only $60,000 prior to 1976. Then if probate is also avoided, the complexities of settling an estate have virtually disappeared — all that must take place is the transfer of assets as per your instructions and the payment of any last bills.

It is unavoidable that you must make the decision as to who will be the executor of your Will and/or the successor trustee under your trust. You are best prepared to make this judgment. With proper planning the responsibilities of the successor trustee or surviving tenant will be minimal and the work for the executor will probably be non-existent. Normally the same person is appointed as successor trustee and executor.

Your successor trustee or surviving tenant will have to 1) pay any final bills from your estate and 2) contact each institution where your assets are held and provide them with a death certificate and/or necessary paperwork. 3) File any necessary last tax returns. The financial institutions will do most of the work. Your representative should only have to follow up to insure the ownership of all assets has been properly transferred. Each institution has a copy of the trust as it was required at the time the account was registered under it. They will distribute assets as instructed.

If assets are held in joint ownership, they will be distributed as the surviving tenant requests. 3) If there is real estate to be sold, or a business to be managed until it is sold, then the successor trustee's duties might become more complex.

Let me emphasize my warning not to appoint a bank or an attorney as successor trustee and/or executor. Do so only under the most unusual circumstances. They will invariably charge at or near the maximum allowed by state statutes. In some 20 states where there is no fee regulation, **any** amount may be charged. Review the example in Chapter 3 where the bank's fee was 38% of the assets of the estate. See Appendix I for a chart of executor's fees allowed by each state's laws. These fees could increase over the years without your knowledge. A period of 10 years or more could pass between the appointment of a bank as executor and your death. During this time period the bank could institute a minimum fee and others unacceptable to you.

We observed from court records that a beneficiary would often receive a handsome fee as executor. Consequently, your assets could be distributed unequally by such maneuvering. Let us take one $270,000 estate as an example. One of the children was the executor and received a fee of $27,000. The Will left everything to the children equally. One child who acted as executor received $108,000 and the other two children received only $81,000.

In another case, the Will stated that the wife was to receive all assets. The executor received a $22,000 fee, and the attorney who handled the legal work received a fee of $45,000.

It is usually wise to have your appointed successor trustee and/or executor serve without a fee. Appoint someone in agreement to this. When there are several beneficiaries, this will help things go smoothly. Everyone will feel they were treated fairly if there is no fee paid to one individual. With good planning, the settling of your estate will require minimal work, and most will feel honored that they have been trusted with this responsibility. Provisions can be made in the trust and Will for appropriate compensation.

Simplify everything for a successor trustee/executor by having the location and account numbers of your assets well organized. Too many bank accounts and assets are never claimed because **heirs do not know that they exist**. Keep a current record of your assets. If an estate or inheritance tax return needs filing, the information needed will be organized for the tax advisor. A book to help organize your records which has been selected for you by the author of this book is offered at the back.

The average commission allowed by the various state laws for an executor is approximately 4% to 5% of the assets and can be as high as 10%. What the statutes allow for the executor's fee is frequently used by attorneys as a guideline for their charges. So, it is easy to see how probate expenses in excess of 10% can occur if 4% to 5% is paid to the attorney plus another 4% to 5% to the executor. This is ridiculous. Attorney fees should be based on work performed, not arbitrarily computed as a fixed percentage of the estate's assets.

Do I Need a Bank or Corporate Trustee?

Rarely. Other authors recommend leaving money with a bank or corporate trustee in charge. Because 70% of the time the husband dies first leaving the wife with all of the business decisions to face on her own, their favorite theme is "the little lady can't handle it emotionally, doesn't have the knowledge, someone might take advantage of her, etc."

Today we find more women making financial decisions. Because this should be a shared responsibility, each spouse should be knowledgeable in the management of their assets. Both should be involved in contact with the family's tax advisor, stockbroker, banker, and attorney. Choose advisors that you believe will best help the surviving spouse.

The best plan is to avoid probate, and to avoid attor-

neys or banks as successor trustee and executor. Many complexities to settle an estate are caused by the complicated
court system. Settlement is easier in the absence of any
federal estate taxes since there is no need to file the 16 page return
for 19 out of 20. Even when these taxes are due, the family's
tax advisor can prepare the returns with information from a currently kept record book.

There is something wrong with a system that takes an
average of 6% - 22% of your life savings, and takes 16 months
to distribute the 78% - 94% left. No court system is going to
be cheap and will invariably be time consuming.

For rare cases where a corporate trustee is necessary, the
best deal I know of is American Guaranty Trust, 3801 Kennett
Pike, Building C-200, Wilmington, Delaware 19807. Telephone,
1-800-441-7698. Their trustee fee is only $100 a year when
$20,000 or more is invested in one of the mutual funds they
manage. Unlike banks, there will not be a continuous parade
of "extra" charges taken out of your money. The Massachusetts
Company, owned by Travelers, provides a similar service as corporate trustee, but their fees are higher. Both are available
through selected stockbrokers. American Guaranty & Trust will
provide you with names of stockbrokers in your area who are
familiar with their services.

American Guaranty Trust **also** draws trust agreements
which saves on attorneys' fees, although they require your own
attorney review any agreements drawn. In addition, they offer
other unique services no bank can. No matter where you might
move, a trust officer is available to you. I know a lady who was
widowed at the age of sixty. She had set up a trust designating
them as her successor trustee. She remarried and moved from
Florida to Idaho. She was pleased that a trust officer came to
see her in Idaho, and he accompanied her to a local attorney
to be sure her trust agreement was in compliance with all Idaho's
statutes. **A definite advantage** of trusts: they are portable. They
can cross state lines as a general rule, requiring no changes. If
you move, it costs less to have an attorney read your trust

as opposed to making a whole new document, which is often necessary with a Will.

No state has any restrictions as to who can be appointed by you as successor trustee. Almost all states have some type of restrictions as to who you can appoint as an executor. Generally, if a nonresident of your state, it has to be a blood relative or relative by marriage or adoption. If you have a question as to who you can appoint as executor in your mind, have your attorney's secretary send you a copy of the probate statutes pertaining to this. Or go by the law library of your county's courthouse and ask the librarian to help you look it up and then make a photostat. Most states require that you be allowed access to the law library - if your taxes have paid for it which they usually do!

A bank as a corporate trustee is often not advisable. If a bank is the **only alternative**, be aware of their charges. Normally the annual fee is .006% of the assets, or a minimum annual of $1,000 and banks issue income checks to beneficiaries on a quarterly basis. If a monthly income is needed, another fee is added for this, one example of the "extra charges" that may appear on your statement. Remember, the income comes to them and you are helpless to stop the parade of charges unless you move your trust. There is usually a fee of 1% to 2% to do that!

One advantage of using a local bank as trustee is the personal contact available with the trust officer. American Guaranty Trust, for example, does not have an officer in every city. You might have to wait a few days before one of their trust officers would be available in person, although one is always available by phone. American Guaranty Trust will provide you with the past investment performance of any of their mutual funds. This information is often difficult to obtain from banks. Offering of the mutual funds managed by the holding company which owns American Guaranty Trust, Delfi Management, Inc., is by prospectus only.

Perhaps I can sum up why I warn against a corporate

or bank as your successor trustee - by now you probably recognize that I sincerely want to help you. You also know something about my credentials - I have been a stockbroker for two prestigious firms that are members of the New York Stock Exchange. And I have two degrees. However, no matter how highly you think of me, would you turn over your checkbook to me? Of course not. Then why would you ever consider turning it over to a bank who is the business of charging fees? It makes no sense unless there is NO relative or friend you can trust.

If you are worried about your successor trustee/executor not doing the absolute right thing by all the beneficiaries, consider making one of your financial advisors co-successor/co-executor. This arrangement requires two signatures. It can be your stockbroker, C. P. A., attorney, etc. Agree to a fee such as $500 or $1,000 and state that this is what has been agreed to in your trust and/or Will. Guard against someone getting a percentage of your savings after your death! The fees suggested are on the premise your relative will do most of the legwork and the co-successor just has to sign some paperwork and verify the figures.

Another alternative, if you have any reservations about who you would like to serve as your successor trustee/executor, is to state in your trust and Will that you wish for your successor trustee/executor to be bonded. For example, on assets of $100,000, a bond typically cost only $300. Call some local bonding companies and inquire about their charges. Or your attorney can find out for you or call the Probate Court for the names of some companies who sell these type bonds. In the 500 probate court cases studied, only 1 in 5 executors was bonded and this was usually because the person died without a Will. Most Wills waive the bond for the executor but where the prudence calls for one, it can be required. Business is business. And the cost is nominal. Probate itself provides no protection the "right" thing will be done. It does GUARANTEE money is going to be LOST to legal and court costs.

Chapter 26

WILLS

A Will is still necessary even if assets have been set up to avoid probate. Distribution of probated assets can be more difficult in the absence of a Will. For instance, miscellaneous checks issued by computers just before or after death must have a court order to have them reissued. A Will provides instructions for the distribution of these checks. As a legal document, properly witnessed and notarized and drawn by an attorney/paralegal, it still has its place, since it instructs your heirs of your wishes. Hopefully, as the Simple Beneficiary Trust becomes popular, financial institutions will accept it for such instructions, but until then make a Will.

The Will given in this chapter is written in "English" as is the Simple Beneficiary Trust. The use of everyday language in legal documents is long overdue for the American public to understand what they are signing. Read your own Will and compare it with this one.

Attorneys use a barrage of archaic and complicated language to camouflage the simplicity of what they do, and help justify their fees. For example, every single Will studied stated, "I nominate, constitute, and appoint XYZ as my executor." All that is necessary is "I appoint." Court approval of the executor named in a Will is required to determine that this person is still capable of handling the estate.

In the following sample Will, the only individually typed words are the names, dates, and places in bold print. "Personal Representative" refers to the executor, which eliminates use of **executor** if male and **executrix** if female:

LAST WILL AND TESTAMENT

of

JANE B. SMITH

I, **JANE B. SMITH**, resident of the City of **Sanford, Seminole** County, Florida, revoke my former Wills and Codicils, or changes to them, and declare this to be my last Will.

I direct my Personal Representative to pay from my estate all the expenses of my last illness, funeral expenses, and other proper charges.

II

I leave my entire estate, and that to which I may become entitled, and over which I may have power of appointment, to my **brother, EDWARD BROWN**, if he predeceases me, then to my **sister-in-law, MARY BROWN**. In the event that both **EDWARD BROWN** and **MARY BROWN** shall predecease me, I leave my entire estate to their children in equal shares. If one child is deceased, then that child's children to share equally in that child's proportionate share. I have intentionally not left anything to my **son, JOHN C. SMITH, JR.,** for reasons known to him.

III

I appoint my **brother, EDWARD BROWN**, as Personal Representative of my estate. In the event he is deceased or unable or unwilling to serve, I appoint my **sister-in-law, MARY BROWN**, as the Personal Representative of my estate. My Personal Representative shall not be required to furnish any bond required under law. I give my Personal Representative full right and power to manage any assets of my estate just as I did when I was alive and mentally competent, without any restrictions, other than to use good judgment as I would:

1. To invest, reinvest, manage, sell, lease, pledge, mortgage, transfer, exchange, convert, or otherwise dispose of, or grant options with respect to any property forming a part of my estate at any time, in such manner, for such purposes, for such prices, and upon such terms, credits or conditions as he may deem advisable.

2. To exercise all powers enumerated in Section 733.612, Florida Statutes, 1977 and this Section is incorporated herein by reference.

My Personal Representative has agreed to serve without compensation unless it is agreed to by all the heirs.

IN WITNESS THEREOF, I sign this 3 page document and declare it my Last Will and Testament on this the _____day of _____, 19_____. This Will is made under FLORIDA State laws and shall be enforced under the laws of that State.

JANE B. SMITH
State of Florida
County of **Seminole**

We, _____, _____,
and **Jane B. Smith,** the **testatrix** (feminine for maker of Will) and the witnesses, respectively, whose names are signed to the attached or foregoing instrument, having been sworn, declared to the undersigned officer that the **testatrix** in the presence of witnesses signed the instrument as her last Will, that she signed, and that each of the witnesses, in the presence of the **testatrix** and in the presence of each other, signed the Will as a witness.

The **testatrix, Jane B. Smith**, stated she signed this Will of her own free will and she appeared to be of sound mind. She also stated she left her son, **John C. Smith, Jr.,** nothing in this Will or by any other means for reasons that are best known to him.

_____

Jane B. Smith(testatrix)

_____

Witness

_____

Witness

Subscribed and sworn to me by **Jane B. Smith**, the **testatrix**, and by _____and _____, the witnesses, on _____, 19_____.

_____

Signature Notary
State of Florida at Large

My commission expires _____

This example looks deceptively easy. Preparing your Will or trust without professional help is not recommended, regardless of books read on the subject or inexpensive forms available to use as your Will. A Will must be notarized and certain wording used to make it "self proving." Self-proving means that it will be accepted as your Will without calling the witnesses in to testify to the validity of your signature. Twenty-two individuals had authored their own Will in the 500 probate cases studied. Many unnecessary problems were caused in 16 of these cases because the Will was poorly worded, or it was not properly executed. Penny-wise and pound-foolish!

In the sample Will, the woman's son would have inherited her assets under the statutes of her state, if she had died without a Will. She chose to leave him nothing, which is her prerogative. If you choose to exclude someone, it is sufficient to state this in your Will or trust. It is not advisable to leave anyone $1 because the executor or successor trustee is required by law to deliver this $1 to the heir. This re-emphasizes that he has been excluded and invites trouble.

Frequently a Will is contested when assets are not left as would have occurred under the states statutes. For example, if your only living relative is a distant cousin you rarely hear from and you decide to leave your assets to charities, this is other than what would have occurred under your state's statutes. The cousin just might appear and contest your Will. Assets can only be distributed after the 2 to 9 months required by law to allow time for anyone to come forward to contest or challenge the validity of a Will, and for creditors to file claims.

As we established in the beginning of this book, it is a myth to believe a Will insures a person's assets avoid probate — yet joint tenancy or a trust do! The primary reason is your estate can be settled in days not allowing any disgruntled parties time to consult their attorneys. Also, they have no way of knowing how much money is involved. They will indeed be able to find out every detail about your assets if your estate goes through probate. Remember, Probate Court records are a matter of "public record." There was not one single case in the probate court files studied where joint tenancy or a trust was contested. These methods not only save an average of 6% - 22% of your assets, but could save substantially more.

If no assets are to be probated, it is not a necessity to file the Will. However, it should be kept for five years. Many probate courts view this as an inconvenience and prefer that the Will not be filed if there are no assets to probate even though state statutes "require it". These same statutes presume there are assets to probate. If the Will is to be filed with the probate court, make several copies. Once the original Will has been given to the probate court, they will permanently retain it and charge you for any copies.

A Will shall prepare your heirs in the event a few miscellaneous checks or other small items have to be dealt with. However, in 49 out of 50 cases, the terrible expense of a probate attorney will not be needed if the advice of this book has been taken!

EPILOGUE

This issue of simplification of the law and change in the legal system involves much more than our subject of avoiding probate. Independent paralegals, for instance, who run secretarial services in the state of Florida, are facing the possibility of prison sentences for "advising" people on legal matters.

The word "advice" has not been legally defined by the legal profession which is attempting to silence them because the establishment of the new independent paralegal profession, no matter how necessary, is a threat to their monopoly and will be precedent setting.

With them, we hope the day will soon come where law is simplified, Judges are elected rather than appointed and nonadversary matters are removed from the courts. Paperwork done by secretaries does not need an attorney's fee attached . . . the American public is tired of paying their "hard earned income" unnecessarily!

Appendix I

COMMISSIONS FOR EXECUTORS AND ADMINISTRATORS

ALABAMA	Commission not to exceed 2 1/2% on receipts and 2 1/2% on money paid out.
ALASKA	Reasonable compensation.
ARIZONA	Reasonable compensation.
ARKANSAS	On personal property: 10% on first $1,000, 5% on next $4,000; 3% of the balance.
CALIFORNIA	4% on first $15,000, 3% of the next $85,000; 2% on next $900,000; 1% on balance over $1 million.
COLORADO	Reasonable compensation.
CONNECTICUT	Reasonable compensation.
DELAWARE	Rates vary.

REPRINTED PERMISSION: Reader's Digest from Family Legal Guide, Chart 18, "Commissions for Executors and Administrators" (partial information).

DISTRICT OF COLUMBIA	Fixed by probate court within limits of 1% to 10% of the inventory value. (Washington, D.C. was visited for our research. Of over 100 files studied, in the majority of cases studied where an executor's fee was awarded, it was 10% or the maximum.)
FLORIDA	Reasonable compensation.
GEORGIA	2 1/2% on monies received and 2 1/2% on money paid out. On property delivered in kind, court may allow reasonable fee up to 3%.
HAWAII	4% of first $15,000 of estate value; 3% of next $85,000; 2% of next $900,000; 1 1/2% of next $2 million; 1% of excess over $3 million; 7% of first $5,000 of estate's yearly income; 5% of balance.
IDAHO	Reasonable compensation.
ILLINOIS	Reasonable compensation. Commission is set by the Probate Court.
INDIANA	Just and reasonable compensation. Commission is set by the Probate Court.
IOWA	6% of the first $1,000, 4% of the next $4,000; 2% of the excess.

KANSAS	Reasonable compensation.
KENTUCKY	May not exceed 5% of personal assets and 5% of income.
LOUISIANA	2 1/2% of inventory value.
MAINE	Not exceeding 5% on the amount of the personal assets.
MARYLAND	Not to exceed 10% on the first $20,000 and 4% on the balance, excluding real estate but not excluding the income thereon. Up to 10% on real estate sold by the executor.
MASSACHUSETTS	As the court may allow. No set rate, but the following are customarily considered not unreasonable: 2 1/2% — 3 1/2% of the personal estate up to $500,000 and 1% of the balance.
MICHIGAN	Reasonable compensation.
MINNESOTA	Reasonable compensation.
MISSISSIPPI	In the discretion of the court, but not to exceed 7% of the entire estate.
MISSOURI	5% on first $5,000 of estate value; 4% on next $20,000; 3% on next $75,000; 2 3/4% on next $300,000; 2 1/2% on next $600,000; 2% on balance over $1 million.

MONTANA	3% on first $40,000 of estate value; 2% on excess over $40,000.
NEBRASKA	Reasonable compensation.
NEVADA	6% on first $1,000, 4% on next $4,000; 2% on excess over $5,000, Sales and services concerning real estate and estate management, are extraordinary services.
NEW HAMPSHIRE	Executor's claim on his accounting is allowed if reasonable.
NEW JERSEY	On estate including real estate: 5% on first $100,000, and not to exceed 5% on excess. 6% on income. Up to 1% more for each additional executor.
NEW MEXICO	Up to 10% on first $3,000; up to 5% of balance, unless otherwise ordered by court. Probate Court sets commission, if any, on real estate.
NEW YORK	For receiving and paying, 5% on first $100,000; 4% on next $200,000; 3% on next $700,000; 2 1/2% on next $4 million; 2% on sums over $5 million.
NORTH CAROLINA	In discretion of court, not exceeding 5% of receipts and expenditures.

NORTH DAKOTA	Reasonable compensation.
OHIO	4% of first $100,000; 3% of $100,000-$400,000; 2% above $400,000.
OKLAHOMA	On entire estate: 5% on first $1,000, 4% on next $4,000, 2 1/2% on excess over $5,000.
OREGON	7% on first $1,000, 4% of next $9,000, 3% of next $40,000, 2% on excess above $50,000. 1% on nonprobate property reportable for tax purposes.
PENNSYLVANIA	No statutory fee, depends upon services performed. In practice, 5% on both principal and income in small estates, 3% in large ones, but no specific dividing line between small and large.
RHODE ISLAND	In the discretion of the court.
SOUTH CAROLINA	2 1/2% on appraised value of personal assets received and 2 1/2% on personal assets paid out plus 10% of interest on money loaned. Probate Court may permit additional compensation for extraordinary services.
SOUTH DAKOTA	5% of first $1,000, 4% of next $4,000; 2 1/2 % of excess over $5,000. Probate Court sets commission on real estate sold.

TENNESSEE	Reasonable compensation.
TEXAS	5% of the gross value of the estate.
UTAH	5% of first $1000, 4% of next $4000, 3% of next $5000, 2% of next $40,000, 1 1/2% of next $50,000, and 1% on excess over $100,000.
VERMONT	Court sets reasonable compensation.
VIRGINIA	Reasonable compensation usually 5%, 2 1/2% on property distributed in kind or in trust.
WASHINGTON	What the court deems just and reasonable.
WASHINGTON, D.C.	See District of Columbia
WEST VIRGINIA	Reasonable compensation, normally 5% on receipts.
WISCONSIN	2% of inventory value less mortgages or liens, plus corpus gains.
WYOMING	10% of first $1000, 5% of next $4,000, 3% of next $15,000, and 2% of excess over $20,000.

Appendix II

ASSET SHEET

ASSET SHEET

Name _____ Date _____

1. FIXED ASSETS

	Amount	Name(s) Held In*
Any excess in checking account	_____	_____
Passbook Savings	_____	_____
Money Market Fund	_____	_____
Money Market Fund	_____	_____
Certificates of Deposit	_____	_____
Certificates of Deposit	_____	_____
Credit Union Accounts	_____	_____
U.S. Savings Bonds	_____	_____
Corporate Bonds/Trusts	_____	_____
Ginnie Mae/Trusts	_____	_____
Tax Exempt Bonds/Trusts	_____	_____
U.S. Treasury or Federal Agency Bonds	_____	_____
Mortgages	_____	_____
Miscellaneous	_____	_____

TOTAL 1. _____

*Single name or only in one name — please list whose name, joint ownership (be sure not tenancy in common), "IN TRUST FOR" at banks or savings & loans, or under your own trust agreement.

2. <u>LIFE INSURANCE & ANNUITIES</u>

	<u>Amount</u>	<u>Beneficiary</u>	<u>Age*</u>
Life Insurance Husband	_____	_____	_____
Life Insurance Wife	_____	_____	_____
Annuities	_____	_____	_____

TOTAL 2. _____

3. <u>VARIABLE ASSETS</u>

	<u>Cost</u>	Market <u>Value</u>	Name(s) Held In
Real Estate	_____	_____	_____
(net equity in home;	_____	_____	_____
market value minus	_____	_____	_____
mortgage)			
Other real estate	_____	_____	_____
(net equity)			
Real Estate Partnerships	_____	_____	_____
	_____	_____	_____

TOTAL 3. _____ _____

*Only to make sure beneficiaries are over 18.
  If under 18, see Chapter 23*

4. <u>STOCKS & BONDS</u>

<u>Name of Company</u>	<u>No. of Shs.</u>	<u>Cost Basis</u>	<u>Market Value</u>	<u>Name(s) Held In</u>
_____	_____	_____	_____	_____
_____	_____	_____	_____	_____
_____	_____	_____	_____	_____
_____	_____	_____	_____	_____
_____	_____	_____	_____	_____

TOTAL 4. _____ _____

5. <u>MISCELLANEOUS</u>

Retirement Plans: Laws concerning these are complex. To determine your total amount of assets, include the entire amount in your retirement plans. If this places you at or near the estate tax limit, seek advice on the portion that would be includable for federal estate and/or state inheritance taxes.

Retirement Plans _____

	<u>Cost</u>	<u>Market Value</u>	<u>Name(s) Held In</u>
Cars	_____	_____	_____
Value of business or practice	_____	_____	_____
Personal property (jewelry, furniture, etc.)	_____	_____	_____
Other	_____	_____	_____

TOTAL 5. _____ _____

<u>TOTAL ESTIMATED ASSETS:</u>

	<u>COST</u>	<u>MARKET VALUE</u>
(Add 1, 2, 3, 4, and 5)	_____	_____

Appendix III

PERSONAL DATA SHEET

INFORMATION SUGGESTED TO TAKE
TO THE ATTORNEY WHO MAKES
YOUR WILL AND/OR TRUST

NAME_____ AGE_____ BIRTHDATE_____

ADDRESS_____ BIRTHPLACE_____

CITY_____ STATE_____ ZIP CODE_____

PHONE NUMBER_____ MARITAL STATUS_____

SOCIAL SEC. #_____ CITIZENSHIP_____

EMPLOYER_____ NO. OF YRS._____

OWN HOME_____ RENT_____ NO. YRS. PRESENT ADDRESS_____

COUNTY YOU ARE A RESIDENT OF_____

MTG. HOLDER_____ MTG.INS. ?_____ INS. CO._____

INTEREST RATE MTG._____ NO. YRS PAY_____ PREPAY PENALTY?_____

STATUS HEALTH & MISC._____

_____

SPOUSE'S NAME_____ BIRTHDATE_____

ADDRESS_____ BIRTHPLACE_____

SOCIAL SEC. #_____ CITIZENSHIP_____

EMPLOYER_____ NO. OF YRS_____

DATE MARRIAGE_____ PLACE MARRIAGE_____

STATUS HEALTH & MISC._____

AGE_____MAIDEN NAME_____

STATUS HEALTH & MISC._____

_____

PREVIOUS MARRIAGE OTHER SPOUSES?_____

CHILDREN FROM THESE MARRIAGES?_____

IF SO, NAMES:_____

_____

CHILDREN:

1. NAME_____ADDRESS_____

    BIRTHDATE_____BIRTHPLACE_____MARITAL STATUS_____

    OCCUPATION_____NAT. OR ADOPTED_____

2. NAME_____ADDRESS_____

    BIRTHDATE_____BIRTHPLACE_____MARITAL STATUS_____

    OCCUPATION_____NAT. OR ADOPTED_____

3. NAME_____ADDRESS_____

    BIRTHDATE_____BIRTHPLACE_____MARITAL STATUS_____

    OCCUPATION_____NAT. OR ADOPTED_____

4. NAME_____ADDRESS_____

    BIRTHDATE_____BIRTHPLACE_____MARITAL STATUS_____

    OCCUPATION_____NAT. OR ADOPTED_____

*Use a separate sheet of write on the back if there are more than 4 children.

DEPENDENTS: (Parents, siblings, etc.)

NAME_____AGE_____BIRTHDATE_____

ADDRESS_____BIRTHPLACE_____

MARITAL STATUS_____RELATIONSHIP_____

SPECIFIC BEQUESTS:

NAME_____AMOUNT OR ITEM_____

ADDRESS_____

PHONE NO._____IF INSTIT. CONTACT?_____

NAME_____AMOUNT OR ITEM_____

ADDRESS_____

PHONE NO._____IF INSTIT. CONTACT?_____

NAME_____AMOUNT OR ITEM_____

ADDRESS_____

PHONE NO._____IF INSTIT. CONTACT?_____

NOTE: If you are having a living trust such as the Simple Beneficiary Trust made, be sure to bring a copy of each bank and brokerage house statement, deeds to property, mortgages and/or promissory notes, etc. with you on your first visit to the attorney. If you hold any actual stock and/or bond certificates, I suggest you let your stockbroker handle re-registering these. The attorney and stockbroker should help you to make sure each and every one of your assets is re-registered under the name of your new trust (only for those having one made). For example, the bank account statement will have to be changed to read:

John Smith, Trustee
Under John Smith Trust Dated 4-17-84
(Or an abbreviated version of the above.)

If the attorney seems inexperienced in all this, then you take the responsibility. See the chapter on each type of asset you own. It will even give you sample letters of instructions to send each institution. Also, be sure to send a copy of your new trust agreement along with the letter which of course should be signed by the present owner(s) of the account. There is normally no charge at the brokerage house to assist you, so you are better off accepting their help and this assures the securities will be done properly. If you don't have a broker, ask friends for the names of theirs who might do this favor on their behalf.

WHEN CHANGES IN OWNERSHIP MUST BE MADE SO YOUR ASSETS AVOID PROBATE, YOU MUST BE SURE THE IN-STITUTION FOLLOWS THE INSTRUCTIONS AND CHANGES THE ACCOUNT OR ASSET TO READ CORRECTLY AS PER THE NAME OF YOUR NEW TRUST OR JOINT OWNERSHIP OR "IN TRUST FOR." COMPUTERS ARE COMPUTERS.

PLEASE ALSO FILL OUT THE ASSET SHEET WHICH IS PER-FORATED, (APPENDIX II), AND TAKE THIS ALSO WITH YOU ON YOUR FIRST VISIT TO THE ATTORNEY WHO IS HELPING YOU WITH ESTATE PLANNING. THE FEES I MENTION ARE SOLELY DEPENDENT ON YOU HAVING ALL THE INFOR-MATION WELL ORGANIZED FOR HIM.

Appendix IV

SAMPLE TRUST FORMAT
FOR CO-TRUSTEES

**FORMAT OF A TRUST FOR CO-TRUSTEES —
meant as an example**. (It is assumed that all children who
are beneficiaries of this trust are over 18. If under 18, or
you do not want them to receive assets until age 25, 30, or
35, discuss with your attorney how to handle this via the
same basic format as follows).

SIMPLE BENEFICIARY TRUST

Trust Agreement

of

Jane B. and John C. Smith

We, Jane B. and John C. Smith, of Baltimore County,
Maryland and being of sound mind, make this Trust Agreement and revoke any other Trust Agreements previously
executed, and any amendments to these prior Trust Agreements.

1. <u>Trust Purpose</u>: Jane B. and John C. Smith hold all assets owned by this Trust for the benefit of their four children and any future or adopted children, to share equally. If one child is deceased or unwilling to receive his share of assets owned by this Trust, that child's share is to go equally to their children. Jane B. and John C. Smith's son, John C. Smith, Jr., is to receive their car(s). Their silver, china, and crystal go to their daughter, Linda Smith Johnson. If John C. Smith, Jr. and/or Linda Smith Johnson, are deceased or unwilling or unable to receive the above items, it is to the Successor Trustee's sole discretion as to who these items go to. It is also to the Successor Trustee's sole discretion as to how any other personal possessions of John C. and/or Jane B. Smith are distributed at their death or in event that they should become incapacitated.

2. <u>Trust Name and Property</u>: Trust shall be known as the "Jane B. and John C. Smith Trust Dated November 17, 1983." Jane B. and John C. Smith are Co-Trustees. Either can transact business for the Trust's assets. All property registered as "Jane B. and John C. Smith Trust Dated 11-17-83" shall be governed by this Trust Agreement. The Grantors (Owners), Jane B. and John C. Smith, have signed separately all paperwork necessary to transfer and deliver to the Trustees all their assets to be held by this Trust, on the following stated terms and conditions as specified herein.

Jane B. and John C. Smith may use any principal and income from assets owned by this Trust to provide for their general comfort, support, health, and education at their sole discretion for as long as they live.

A Successor Trustee is named in the event Jane B. and John C. Smith are incapacitated as defined. At the death of Jane B. and John C. Smith, the Successor Trustee is to distribute the assets owned by this Trust and this Trust terminates.

3. <u>Successor Trustee</u>: If both Jane B. and John C. Smith are physically or mentally incapacitated, as certified in writing by two licensed physicians or are deceased, the Successor Trustee shall be James D. Brown, Jane B. Smith's father. If he is deceased or unable or unwilling to serve, then Frank E. Smith, John C. Smith's father, is asked to serve. The Successor Trustee agrees to serve with no compensation unless otherwise agreed to by the beneficiaries.

The Trustee or any Successor Trustee may expend income and/or principal to provide for the health, education, support, and general welfare of Jane B. and/or John C. Smith in the manner of living in which they are accustomed.

If Jane B. Smith and/or John C. Smith are incapacitated, as certified in writing by two licensed physicians, their Successor Trustee may, on their behalf, employ or terminate physicians, nurses, nursing homes, hospital and others at his/her discretion for Jane B. Smith and/or John C. Smith's care. Any Successor Trustee may sign instructions and consents as required by an attending physician, hospital or nursing home, etc.

4. <u>Management</u>: Jane B. and/or John C. Smith, the Co-Trustees, or any Successor Trustee, shall have all the powers that Jane B. and/or John C. Smith would have if she/he were mentally competent, and still owned the assets only in her/his name. Management of the assets owned by this Trust shall be at either of the Co-Trustee's or Successor Trustee's sole discretion. This includes the right to borrow against or pledge any of the assets, and the right to mortgage any real estate or margin stocks.

5. <u>Right to Revoke or Change</u>: Jane B. and/or John C. Smith reserve the right to revoke, amend or make changes to this Trust at any point during their lifetime.

6. <u>Creditors</u>: The assets owned by this Trust are not accessible in any way by creditors of their beneficiaries, Successor Trustee, or their past or present spouses.

7. <u>Bond and Accounting</u>: No bond shall be required of the Trustees or any Successor Trustee. Jane B. and/or John C. Smith delegate any accounting of the Trust's assets to the sole discretion of any Successor Trustee, and they need not comply with any of the provisions of the Trust accounting statutes of Maryland as they presently exist or may be amended, or any new statutes in this regard. (Optional: When there are several beneficiaries, you could request that your Sucessor Trustee have a tax advisor send them accounting statements specifying amounts and the source.)

8. <u>Taxes & Debts</u>: The Successor Trustee can pay from assets of the Trust debts and taxes of Jane B. Smith and/or John C. Smith he deems proper and reasonable.

9. <u>Disappearance</u>: If Jane B. and John C. Smith should disappear, the Successor Trustee shall manage the assets as provided by this Trust. If they are not heard from for two years, and their bodies are not recovered, all the assets are to be distributed as provided in this Trust Agreement.

This trust was executed in triplicate in Maryland and shall be enforced under the laws of the state of Maryland. Any copies signed and executed by Jane B. Smith shall be treated the same as an original.

Jane B. Smith	John C. Smith

We witnessed Jane B. Smith and John C. Smith sign this Trust Agreement in triplicate on 17 November 1983, and witnessed each others signatures at their request. We also attest that they appeared to be of sound mind; and signed this Trust Agreement of their own free will.

Witness: _____   Witness: _____

Address: _____   Address: _____

_____   _____
City   State   City   State

STATE OF MARYLAND
COUNTY OF _____

NOTARY: Jane B. Smith and John C. Smith, who appeared before me and who were duly sworn, signed this Trust Agreement. They stated they did so of their own free will, and appeared to be of sound mind.

WITNESS my hand and official seal, this _____day of _____A.D. 19_____.

_____
Signature Notary
State of Maryland at Large

My commission expires _____

Appendix V

REVOCATION OF TRUST AGREEMENT

When the decision has been made to revoke a trust, assets should be re-registered as soon as possible in order to remove the name of the revoked trust from each asset registered under it. **A revocation is necessary only if you are not making a new trust agreement which includes revoking any prior trust agreements.** It is a necessity to promptly follow through with re-registering assets under the new trust or back to some other type of ownership if only a revocation is done and a new trust is not drawn.

REVOCATION OF TRUST AGREEMENT

This Revocation is made this _____ day of _____ 19_____ by _____.
A declaration of Revocable Trust dated_____
was created by me in writing. Assets of the Trust were
_____
_____
_____and the beneficiaries were
_____
_____.

By the terms of the Trust, I reserved the full power and right to revoke the Trust without the consent of the beneficiaries and choose to do so. Attached is a copy of the Trust.

Pursuant to the power and right of revocation, I do hereby revoke the above Trust in its entirety and discharge the Trust property and all the terms and provisions of the Trust known as the _____.

_____   _____
            Witness   Signature Creator

_____

Witness

Notary: _____, who appeared before me on _____ and was duly sworn, signed this Revocation. He appeared to do so of his own free will and to be of sound mind.

WITNESS my hand and official seal, this _____ day of _____ A. D. 19_____.

STATE OF _____
COUNTY OF _____

                              _____

                              Signature Notary

                              State of _____ at Large

My commission expires _____

GENERAL GLOSSARY
of PROBATE TERMS

accumulation trust: a trust in which the income may in whole or in part be retained in trust instead of being distributed to the beneficiaries.

administration: the period of time after a decedent's death when his affairs are handled under the court's supervision; often synonymous with probate.

administrator: the court appointed person handling an administration when there was no Will that named an executor. Feminine: administratrix.

alternate valuation date: a date six months after a decedent's death that, when elected, allows all of the assets of his estate to be valued.

ancillary: what probate court proceedings are called if real estate and sometimes other types of property is owned in a state other than your state of residence or domicile. The entire probate process including all the burdens and cost must be executed in the other states.

annual exclusion: the sum of $10,000 (each) which may be given by a person as a gift to one or more individuals every year, free of federal gift tax.

attorney-in-fact: the agent or person granted the right to act under a power-of-attorney.

basis: capital gain is the excess of selling price over the cost basis. It is usually an asset's cost, but may be later adjusted.

beneficiary: the person to receive the assets of a trust or for whom it is managed. Also, the recipient of life insurance proceeds, benefit plans, or gifts in a Will.

bond: a guarantee by an insurance or similar company agreeing to make up for any loss negligently or criminally done by an executor or administrator.

buy-sell agreement: an agreement among co-owners of a business promising to buy out one at death or other occurrences.

by-pass trust: a trust designed to avoid estate taxes at the death of the person who retains a lifetime interest in that trust.

capacity: see Testamentary Capacity.

capital gain: the profit realized by the sale of capital assets owned for more than one year.

chancery court: in some states, what the probate court is called.

Clifford Trust: a trust lasting more than ten years, after which the original creator of the trust gets the property back.

closely held corporation: a corporation the shares of which are not traded on any recognized stock exchange, so are "closely held."

codicil: a document making a change to or supplementing a Will.

community property: all property acquired in one of the 8 community property states by married persons during marriage that is not separate property; the earnings or fruits of the marriage. The eight state are: Arizona, California, Idaho, Louisiana, Nevada, New Mexico, Texas, and Washington.

conservatorship: available in some states, it resembles a guardianship of an incompetent, but without the stigma of incompetency.

contest: see Will contest.

contribution theory: the rule under which joint tenancy property is taxed, based upon the contributions of the decedent.

corpus: the property owned by a trust; synonymous with Principal.

Court Trust: a trust that is subject to the ongoing jurisdiction of the probate court.

creditor's claim: a document that must be filed by a decedent's creditors in order to get paid from the assets of his estate.

Curtesy: the reverse of Dower (see Dower); a husband's rights.

decedent: a person who has died.

deductions: items that may be subtracted from taxable income, the taxable estate, or taxable gifts, thereby lowering the amount on which the tax is due.

devise and bequeath: ancient words meaning to pass property by Will.

discretionary trust: a trust that allows the trustee to distribute the annual income of a trust among such persons as he sees fit.

Donor: the person who gives property or who gives a power of appointment.

domicile: a legal term fixing the state or country within which a decedent's estate will be probated and taxed; it is where he intended his permanent home to be.

donee: the person to whom a Power of Appointment, or any other property, is given.

dower: increasingly outmoded term for the percentage share of marital property automatically given to a wife upon the death of her husband; applies only in Common Law states.

durable power-of-attorney: legal document granting another the right to act on your behalf even if you are incapacitated. In some states this type oof power-of-attoreny is null and void if you have been declared legally incompetent.

Economic Recovery Tax Act of 1981: it raised federal estate tax exemptions and tax-free gift amounts, lowered rates, and introduced the unlimited marital deduction.

election: a choice or option to select among different alternatives.

escheat: when a person dies intestate (without a Will) and there are no heirs, it goes to the state; it "escheats".

estate tax: the death tax imposed by the federal government and some states on the assets (estate) of a decedent, taxing the decedent's privilege of leaving his property to others at his death.

executor: the person named in a Will to handle the probate administration under court supervision. Feminine: executrix.

exemption: a certain minimum amount on which tax does not apply.

family allowance: (sometimes called "widow's allowance") an amount allowed by a probate court for the support of a surviving spouse and often, also minor children.

fee simple: ownership of property in one name, unburdened by any further interest or any possibility of losing total ownership.

fiduciary: a person acting for another under the highest possible standards, such as executors, trustees, guardians, etc.

fiduciary income tax return: the tax return that must be filed by an estate, some trusts, or any other entity managed by a fiduciary.

funded trust: a living trust that has assets re-registered under it. Avoids probate.

general power of appointment: a power wherein appointment may be made to anyone at all, including the power holder himself, his creditors, etc. (See power of appointment.

gift tax: an excise tax on the privilege of making gifts.

gifts to minors act: see Uniform Gifts to Minors Act.

Grantor: the Creator (owner of assets transferred to a trust); synonymous with Settlor and Trustor.

gross estate: the total property that can be taxed by an estate tax.

guardianship: court supervised administration of the property and/or person of either a minor child or an incompetent adult.

heir: anyone taking property under a Will or succeeding to property by intestacy (without a Will).

Holographic Will: permitted only in some states, it is a Will entirely in the handwriting of the Testator (maker).

Individual Retirement Accounts (IRAs): retirement funds allowed to any income earner up to $2,000 per year, tax deductible ($2,250 per year if the spouse is not employed).

inheritance tax: a tax imposed by many states on the privilege of inheriting property. Imposed on the recipient, not on the decedent.

inter vivos: Latin for "during life;" describes a trust or anything else established or done during a person's lifetime.

intestacy: the state of dying without a valid Will. State law then determines who inherits the property.

intestate: a person who dies without leaving a valid Will.

inventory: a probate court document listing, and often valuing, all the property contained in the probate estate.

irrevocable trust: a trust that may never be revoked or amended by its creator.

issue: all persons who have descended from an ancestor in a direct lineal line; your children, grandchildren, great-grandchildren, etc.

joint and mutual Will: a single Will signed by both husband and wife, disposing of their property at each death. Usually to be avoided.

joint tenancy: co-ownership between two or more people with right of survivorship, meaning that a survivor automatically becomes the owner of a decedent's interest. Avoids probate.

Joint Tenancy with Right of Survivorship: see joint tenancy.

Keogh Plans: retirement plans for self-employed persons and partners (named after the Congressman who introduced them).

legacy: a gift of property in a Will; usually refers to a gift of cash.

Letters Testamentary: what many states call the document that evidences the authority of an executor to act for his decedent's estate.

life estate: the right to use and enjoy property during someone's lifetime with the property owned by someone else.

life tenant: the person who is in possession of a life estate, or life interest in a trust.

living trust: same as Inter Vivos Trust; a trust created during one's lifetime.

marital deduction: allows a decedent spouse a deduction from death taxes for all property left to the surviving spouse. Now an unlimited amount for federal estate taxes.

no contest clause: a clause in a Will attempting to disinherit any person who attacks the Will's legal validity.

noncourt trust: a trust that is not subject to the ongoing jurisdiction of a probate court; opposite of Court Trust. For example: a Simple Beneficiary Trust.

notice to creditors: informing a decedent's creditors that he has died, and that they should enter their claims against his estate.

Nuncupative Will: an oral Will, only allowed in some states for a small amount of Personal Property, and usually only if made a limited number of days before death.

orphan's court: in some states what the probate court is called.

owner (of insurance): the person who possesses all of the Incidents of Ownership in an insurance policy.

partition: a court proceeding allowing any joint or co-owner of property to force a separation of the interests, usually by a court ordered auction sale with the proceeds divided among the owners.

per capita: describes sharing an inheritance in equal shares by relatives in an equal degree of relationship to a decedent.

per stirpes: latin for "by stocks"; a deceased child's children share his proportion equally.

personal property: all tangible or intangible property which is not real property (real estate).

personal representative: best term for a person handling an estate during administration under the probate court's supervision; includes both executors and administrators.

pour-over Will or trust: a Will (the "pour-over Will") that leaves property to an already existing living trust (the "pour-over trust").

power of appointment: the power to designate who shall be the owner of property. Subheadings: general and special powers.

power-of-attorney: legal document granting another the right to act for you (general or specific). Becomes null and void if maker is incapacitated.

preliminary distribution: a distribution of some of the property in an estate before the estate is ready to be closed.

pretermitted child: a child unintentionally omitted from all mention in the Will of its parents, often entitled to a statutory share.

principal: the property comprising a trust; synonymous with Corpus and Res.

probate: administration of a decedent's affairs and handled under court supervision until the assets are distributed. Synonymous with Administration.

probate court: the branch of a state's regular court where probate matters are handled. Probate "matters" are guardianships and transfer to heirs — primarily assets, only in the decedent's name which are governed by a Will or the state's laws if there is no Will.

Q-Tip Trust: a type of trust that will qualify for the marital deduction.

real property: land or real estate, together with whatever is growing or erected on it or affixed to it.

remainder: the property interest passing to a new owner after a life estate or other interim interest has come to end usually by the death of the person having the life estate.

remainderman: the person who will acquire the remainder. See remainder.

residence: to be differentiated from Domicile. Where one currently lives, but not necessarily one's Domicile.

residuary clause: the clause in a Will disposing of the residue. See residue.

residue: all the property left to be disposed or by Will or trust after specific items have been given to specific persons.

revocable trust: a trust that may at any time be revoked, amended or changed by its creator.

revocation: document terminating a trust agreement.

right of representation: describes dividing an inheritance (not necessarily equal shares) when heirs "represent" a predeceased relative and share whatever that relative would have been entitled to.

right of survivorship: part of the definition of Joint Tenancy ownership, it means that the surviving joint tenant will automatically become the owner of the property when the other joint tenant(s) dies.

self-proving: in most states, a Will can have certain wording incorporated in the notary's statement attesting to the validity of your signature. Eliminates the calling of witnesses to testify at your death. A detail overlooked by the majority of people who make their own Will.

Settlor: the person who creates a trust: synonymous with Trustor and Grantor.

severance: the breaking of a Joint Tenancy (becomes Tenancy in Common) when one of the joint tenants does one of many acts making it inequitable to continue as a joint tenancy.

Simple Beneficiary Trust: a living, revocable, amendable (changeable) trust established during the maker's lifetime. The primary purpose of this type of trust is to have assets avoid probate by designating beneficiaries**while you are living**to receive your assets at your death and to provide for a successor trustee (if you choose) in case you are incapacitated.

special power of appointment: a power where appointment is restricted to a designated class or group of named persons.

spendthrift clause: a protective trust clause stating that the beneficiary's interest may not be attacked by his creditor or taken in bankruptcy.

sprinkling trust: synonymous with a discretionary trust; the trustee can "sprinkle" the income among various beneficiaries.

stepped-up basis: provision whereby heir's cost basis in inherited property is equal to its value at the date of the death.

stock/bond powers: written authorization separate from a certificate granting permission to transfer a security. Useless unless it is attached to the actual certificate. (Like any power-of-attorney, it is made null and void by death.)

Successor Trustee: the person or institution who takes over the management of assets if you are incapacitated and distributes the assets owned by the trust at your death or continues the management of the assets or behalf of beneficiaries i.e. minors (children under 18).

surrogate court: what some states call their probate court.

Tenancy by the Entirety: essentially identical to a Joint Tenancy with Right of Survivorship but only for husband and wife. Avoids probate.

Tenancy in Common: co-ownership between two or more people where each tenant owns a defined percentage of the whole. Does not avoid probate.

ten-year trust: synonymous with Clifford Trust; see that definition.

testamentary capacity: the legal capacity to make a Will.

testamentary trust: a trust, created in a Will, that does not come into existence until after the maker's death. Assets must go through probate before they can be placed in the trust.

testate: leaving a valid Will, as opposed to dying intestate (without a Will).

testator: the person who writes and executes a will. Feminine: testatrix.

303 redemption: a purchase of closely held stock by the corporation itself in amounts sufficient to pay the stockholder's federal and state death taxes and administration expenses.

Totten Trusts: special banking arrangements where the depositor holds the account "in trust for" another and retains sole ownership of the funds for the rest of his, the depositor's life. The instructions that can be given are who the beneficiaries are at the death of the depositor.

Trust: a legal entity in which one person (the trustee) or institution holds and manages property for the benefit of someone else.

Trustee: the person who holds trust property for the benefit of themselves and/or another — the beneficiaries.

Trustor: the person who creates a trust; synonymous with Settlor and Grantor.

undivided interest: the percentage interest held by a Tenant in Common.

unfunded trust: a living trust in which assets have not been re-registered under it.

Uniform Gifts to Minors Acts: a uniform act in force in most states, enabling a gift of specified types of property to a Custodian who holds the assets for a minor until the minor comes of age.

Uniform Probate Code: a uniform act adopted in 14 states and in part by most states that attempts to reduce a court's involvement in the probate process. It has been of little success at simplifying the process or making it less costly.

unlimited marital deduction: allows one spouse to transfer an unlimited amount of property to the other spouse, completely free of transfer tax, either during life or at death.

widow's election: a device found mostly in community property states where one spouse wants to dispose of the property belonging to the other spouse, giving the survivor and option as to whether or not to go along with that attempt.

Will: a formal document directing the disposal or distribution of one's property after his death. Does not avoid probate.

Will contest: legal proceedings to overturn a decedent's Will for lack of testamentary capacity or lack of due execution.

INDEX

B

C

ORDER FORM

SATISFACTION GUARANTEED or your money
back in 30 days if returned in resalable
condition -- **you take NO RISK!**
MAKE YOUR CHECK PAYABLE TO:
LINCH PUBLISHING, INC.
Box 75
Orlando, FL 32802
1-407-647-3025
(check or money order only)

All of our books are available through B. Dalton Booksellers, Walden-
books and other fine bookstores. Have them look up the book you wish
under the author's name as they often have trouble finding it under the
titles. Tell any bookstore you contact they may obtain our books
through their distributor **INGRAM.**

Item	Number	Amount
_____	_____	_____
_____	_____	_____
_____	_____	_____

$2 for each for item for postage & handling   _____

Florida residents add 6% sales tax   _____

                              TOTAL: $_____

NAME:_____

Address:_____

City:_____State_____Zip_____

Telephone No.: (_____)_____

The Simple Beneficiary Trust (Personal Trust) is often recommended by Barbara Stock
for those who are single, widowed or divorced, for married couples who have
reached their 60's (most may have a Joint Trust), for marriages where you wish
children by a prior marriage to receive part or all of your assets, if the health of one
spouse has failed, or if your assets will be subject to Federal Estate Taxes. The
AVOIDING PROBATE FORMS KIT contains all the forms necessary: Living Trust
Forms to fit any situation, Special Will to go with the Trust (Pour-Over), Durable
Powers of Attorney, Bill of Sale Personal Possessions to the Trust, etc. Also, included are all types of regular Wills including one with a Trust for your children, which
are appropriate for couples who are ages 18 to 59, who have decided to stick with
joint ownership, or for those in California who have countable assets of less than
$60,000. All forms sold are used on a regular basis by attorneys. Also, available is
an audio tape of Barbara Stock and one of the five attorneys who helped make the
forms, conducting an actual class on how to fill out the same forms in our Kit-
$16.95. The **AVOIDING PROBATE FORMS KIT** -- $39.95 (with all the instructions
necessary) and tape, if ordered together, are only $49.95 plus $2 each for ptg. and
hdlg. or $53.95 and if a Florida resident, add 6% sales tax (total FL $56.35). Failure
to enclose the appropriate postage and handling or sales tax will delay your order as
we will have to write to you to request it.

ORDER FORM

SATISFACTION GUARANTEED or your money
back in 30 days if returned in resalable
condition -- **you take NO RISK!**

MAKE YOUR CHECK PAYABLE TO:
LINCH PUBLISHING, INC.

Box 75
Orlando, FL 32802
1-407-647-3025
(check or money order only)

All of our books are available through B. Dalton Booksellers, Walden-books and other fine bookstores. Have them look up the book you wish under the author's name as they often have trouble finding it under the titles. Tell any bookstore you contact they may obtain our books through their distributor **INGRAM**.

Item	Number	Amount
_____	_____	_____
_____	_____	_____
_____	_____	_____
$2 for each for item for postage & handling		_____
Florida residents add 6% sales tax		_____
TOTAL:		$_____

NAME:_____

Address:_____

City:_____State_____Zip_____

Telephone No.: (____)_____

The Simple Beneficiary Trust (Personal Trust) is often recommended by Barbara Stock for those who are single, widowed or divorced, for married couples who have reached their 60's (most may have a Joint Trust), for marriages where you wish children by a prior marriage to receive part or all of your assets, if the health of one spouse has failed, or if your assets will be subject to Federal Estate Taxes. The **AVOIDING PROBATE FORMS KIT** contains all the forms necessary: Living Trust Forms to fit any situation, Special Will to go with the Trust (Pour-Over), Durable Powers of Attorney, Bill of Sale Personal Possessions to the Trust, etc. Also, includ-ed are all types of regular Wills including one with a Trust for your children, which are appropriate for couples who are ages 18 to 59, who have decided to stick with joint ownership, or for those in California who have countable assets of less than $60,000. All forms sold are used on a regular basis by attorneys. Also, available is an audio tape of Barbara Stock and one of the five attorneys who helped make the forms, conducting an actual class on how to fill out the same forms in our Kit-$16.95. The **AVOIDING PROBATE FORMS KIT** -- $39.95 (with all the instructions necessary) and tape, if ordered together, are only $49.95 plus $2 each for ptg. and hdlg. or $53.95 and if a Florida resident, add 6% sales tax (total FL $56.35). Failure to enclose the appropriate postage and handling or sales tax will delay your order as we will have to write to you to request it.

ORDER FORM
SATISFACTION GUARANTEED or your money back in 30 days if returned in resalable condition -- **you take NO RISK!**
MAKE YOUR CHECK PAYABLE TO:
LINCH PUBLISHING, INC.
Box 75
Orlando, FL 32802
1-407-647-3025
(check or money order only)

All of our books are available through B. Dalton Booksellers, Waldenbooks and other fine bookstores. Have them look up the book you wish under the author's name as they often have trouble finding it under the titles. Tell any bookstore you contact they may obtain our books through their distributor **INGRAM.**

Item	Number	Amount
_____	_____	_____
_____	_____	_____
_____	_____	_____

$2 for each for item for postage & handling   _____

Florida residents add 6% sales tax   _____

TOTAL: $_____

NAME:_____

Address:_____

City:_____State_____Zip_____

Telephone No.: (____)_____

The Simple Beneficiary Trust (Personal Trust) is often recommended by Barbara Stock for those who are single, widowed or divorced, for married couples who have reached their 60's (most may have a Joint Trust), for marriages where you wish children by a prior marriage to receive part or all of your assets, if the health of one spouse has failed, or if your assets will be subject to Federal Estate Taxes. The **AVOIDING PROBATE FORMS KIT** contains all the forms necessary: Living Trust Forms to fit any situation, Special Will to go with the Trust (Pour-Over), Durable Powers of Attorney, Bill of Sale Personal Possessions to the Trust, etc. Also, included are all types of regular Wills including one with a Trust for your children, which are appropriate for couples who are ages 18 to 59, who have decided to stick with joint ownership, or for those in California who have countable assets of less than $60,000. All forms sold are used on a regular basis by attorneys. Also, available is an audio tape of Barbara Stock and one of the five attorneys who helped make the forms, conducting an actual class on how to fill out the same forms in our Kit- $16.95. The **AVOIDING PROBATE FORMS KIT** -- $39.95 (with all the instructions necessary) and tape, if ordered together, are only $49.95 plus $2 each for ptg. and hdlg. or $53.95 and if a Florida resident, add 6% sales tax (total FL $56.35). Failure to enclose the appropriate postage and handling or sales tax will delay your order as we will have to write to you to request it.

ORDER FORM

SATISFACTION GUARANTEED or your money
back in 30 days if returned in resalable
condition -- **you take NO RISK!**

MAKE YOUR CHECK PAYABLE TO:
LINCH PUBLISHING, INC.

Box 75
Orlando, FL 32802
1-407-647-3025
(check or money order only)

All of our books are available through B. Dalton Booksellers, Walden-books and other fine bookstores. Have them look up the book you wish under the author's name as they often have trouble finding it under the titles. Tell any bookstore you contact they may obtain our books through their distributor **INGRAM**.

Item	Number	Amount
_____	_____	_____
_____	_____	_____
_____	_____	_____

$2 for each for item for postage & handling _____

Florida residents add 6% sales tax _____

TOTAL: $_____

NAME:_____

Address:_____

City:_____State_____Zip_____

Telephone No.: (____)_____

The Simple Beneficiary Trust (Personal Trust) is often recommended by Barbara Stock for those who are single, widowed or divorced, for married couples who have reached their 60's (most may have a Joint Trust), for marriages where you wish children by a prior marriage to receive part or all of your assets, if the health of one spouse has failed, or if your assets will be subject to Federal Estate Taxes. The **AVOIDING PROBATE FORMS KIT** contains all the forms necessary: Living Trust Forms to fit any situation, Special Will to go with the Trust (Pour-Over), Durable Powers of Attorney, Bill of Sale Personal Possessions to the Trust, etc. Also, included are all types of regular Wills including one with a Trust for your children, which are appropriate for couples who are ages 18 to 59, who have decided to stick with joint ownership, or for those in California who have countable assets of less than $60,000. All forms sold are used on a regular basis by attorneys. Also, available is an audio tape of Barbara Stock and one of the five attorneys who helped make the forms, conducting an actual class on how to fill out the same forms in our Kit- $16.95. The **AVOIDING PROBATE FORMS KIT** -- $39.95 (with all the instructions necessary) and tape, if ordered together, are only $49.95 plus $2 each for ptg. and hdlg. or $53.95 and if a Florida resident, add 6% sales tax (total FL $56.35). Failure to enclose the appropriate postage and handling or sales tax will delay your order as we will have to write to you to request it.

ORDER FORM

MAKE YOUR CHECK PAYABLE TO:
LINCH PUBLISHING, INC.

Box 75
Orlando, FL 32802
1-407-647-3025
(check or money order only)

All of our books are available through B. Dalton Booksellers, Walden-
books and other fine bookstores. Have them look up the book you wish
under the author's name as they often have trouble finding it under the
titles. Tell any bookstore you contact they may obtain our books
through their distributor **INGRAM.**

Item	Number	Amount
_____	_____	_____
_____	_____	_____
_____	_____	_____
$2 for each for item for postage & handling		_____
Florida residents add 6% sales tax		_____
	TOTAL:	$_____

NAME:_____

Address:_____

City:_____State_____Zip_____

Telephone No.: (____)_____

The Simple Beneficiary Trust (Personal Trust) is often recommended by Barbara Stock
for those who are single, widowed or divorced, for married couples who have
reached their 60's (most may have a Joint Trust), for marriages where you wish
children by a prior marriage to receive part or all of your assets, if the health of one
spouse has failed, or if your assets will be subject to Federal Estate Taxes. The
AVOIDING PROBATE FORMS KIT contains all the forms necessary: Living Trust
Forms to fit any situation, Special Will to go with the Trust (Pour-Over), Durable
Powers of Attorney, Bill of Sale Personal Possessions to the Trust, etc. Also, included are all types of regular Wills including one with a Trust for your children, which
are appropriate for couples who are ages 18 to 59, who have decided to stick with
joint ownership, or for those in California who have countable assets of less than
$60,000. All forms sold are used on a regular basis by attorneys. Also, available is
an audio tape of Barbara Stock and one of the five attorneys who helped make the
forms, conducting an actual class on how to fill out the same forms in our Kit-
$16.95. The **AVOIDING PROBATE FORMS KIT** -- $39.95 (with all the instructions
necessary) and tape, if ordered together, are only $49.95 plus $2 each for ptg. and
hdlg. or $53.95 and if a Florida resident, add 6% sales tax (total FL $56.35). Failure
to enclose the appropriate postage and handling or sales tax will delay your order as
we will have to write to you to request it.

ORDER FORM

SATISFACTION GUARANTEED or your money
back in 30 days if returned in resalable
condition -- **you take NO RISK!**
MAKE YOUR CHECK PAYABLE TO:
LINCH PUBLISHING, INC.
Box 75
Orlando, FL 32802
1-407-647-3025
(check or money order only)

All of our books are available through B. Dalton Booksellers, Walden-
books and other fine bookstores. Have them look up the book you wish
under the author's name as they often have trouble finding it under the
titles. Tell any bookstore you contact they may obtain our books
through their distributor **INGRAM.**

Item	Number	Amount
_____	_____	_____
_____	_____	_____
_____	_____	_____

$2 for each for item for postage & handling   _____
 Florida residents add 6% sales tax   _____

                          TOTAL: $_____

NAME:_____

Address:_____

City:_____State_____Zip_____

Telephone No.: (____)_____

   The Simple Beneficiary Trust (Personal Trust) is often recommended by Barbara Stock
for those who are single, widowed or divorced, for married couples who have
reached their 60's (most may have a Joint Trust), for marriages where you wish
children by a prior marriage to receive part or all of your assets, if the health of one
spouse has failed, or if your assets will be subject to Federal Estate Taxes. The
AVOIDING PROBATE FORMS KIT contains all the forms necessary: Living Trust
Forms to fit any situation, Special Will to go with the Trust (Pour-Over), Durable
Powers of Attorney, Bill of Sale Personal Possessions to the Trust, etc. Also, included are all types of regular Wills including one with a Trust for your children, which
are appropriate for couples who are ages 18 to 59, who have decided to stick with
joint ownership, or for those in California who have countable assets of less than
$60,000. All forms sold are used on a regular basis by attorneys. Also, available is
an audio tape of Barbara Stock and one of the five attorneys who helped make the
forms, conducting an actual class on how to fill out the same forms in our Kit-
$16.95. The **AVOIDING PROBATE FORMS KIT** -- $39.95 (with all the instructions
necessary) and tape, if ordered together, are only $49.95 plus $2 each for ptg. and
hdlg. or $53.95 and if a Florida resident, add 6% sales tax (total FL $56.35). Failure
to enclose the appropriate postage and handling or sales tax will delay your order as
we will have to write to you to request it.

ORDER FORM
SATISFACTION GUARANTEED or your money
back in 30 days if returned in resalable
condition -- you take NO RISK!
MAKE YOUR CHECK PAYABLE TO:
LINCH PUBLISHING, INC.
Box 75
Orlando, FL 32802
1-407-647-3025
(check or money order only)

All of our books are available through B. Dalton Booksellers, Walden-books and other fine bookstores. Have them look up the book you wish under the author's name as they often have trouble finding it under the titles. Tell any bookstore you contact they may obtain our books through their distributor **INGRAM**.

Item	Number	Amount
_____	_____	_____
_____	_____	_____
_____	_____	_____

$2 for each for item for postage & handling   _____

Florida residents add 6% sales tax   _____

TOTAL: $_____

NAME:_____

Address:_____

City:_____State_____Zip_____

Telephone No.: (____)_____

The Simple Beneficiary Trust (Personal Trust) is often recommended by Barbara Stock for those who are single, widowed or divorced, for married couples who have reached their 60's (most may have a Joint Trust), for marriages where you wish children by a prior marriage to receive part or all of your assets, if the health of one spouse has failed, or if your assets will be subject to Federal Estate Taxes. The **AVOIDING PROBATE FORMS KIT** contains all the forms necessary: Living Trust Forms to fit any situation, Special Will to go with the Trust (Pour-Over), Durable Powers of Attorney, Bill of Sale Personal Possessions to the Trust, etc. Also, included are all types of regular Wills including one with a Trust for your children, which are appropriate for couples who are ages 18 to 59, who have decided to stick with joint ownership, or for those in California who have countable assets of less than $60,000. All forms sold are used on a regular basis by attorneys. Also, available is an audio tape of Barbara Stock and one of the five attorneys who helped make the forms, conducting an actual class on how to fill out the same forms in our Kit- $16.95. The **AVOIDING PROBATE FORMS KIT** -- $39.95 (with all the instructions necessary) and tape, if ordered together, are only $49.95 plus $2 each for ptg. and hdlg. or $53.95 and if a Florida resident, add 6% sales tax (total FL $56.35). Failure to enclose the appropriate postage and handling or sales tax will delay your order as we will have to write to you to request it.